STRONG GIRL, BRAVE GIRL

A SINGLE MOTHER'S CANDID
STORY OF RECONCILING A LIFE
UNEXPECTED AND NAVIGATING
THE MESSY IN-BETWEEN

————

KELSEY BALDWIN

PUBLISHED IN SPRINGFIELD, MISSOURI

ISBN 978-1-7326279-0-1 (paperback)
ISBN 978-1-7326279-1-8 (ebook)

Cover artwork by Penelope Baldwin
Book design by Kelsey Baldwin
Edited by Alicia Kelley

For more information about this book, visit www.paperandoats.com/book.

For my little bird.

Bear with me a little longer and I will show you
that there is more to be said in God's behalf.

JOB 36:2 (NIV)

CONTENTS

THE MiDDLE

"And when you go wondering where you will go or what will happen next,
keep your eyes fixed above; you are far from finished yet."

MORGAN HARPER NICHOLS

There's that moment just before a plane lands when you find yourself anxiously praying that it comes back down to Earth safely. You can't fathom how this huge flying Tylenol, going 500 mph, will be casually rolling up to the gate in just three minutes. My dad traveled a lot when I was a kid, and so he became a frequent flyer who knew all the tricks. He told me once that it takes exactly three minutes from the time the wheels come out from the belly of the plane until they touch the runway. And so, on every flight I've ever taken, I start counting to 180 as soon as I hear the hatch open under my feet.

The first few times I counted, it was exactly three minutes, and I thought my dad must be some kind of wizard. And as flights went by, it was more like two minutes or four or five, or maybe the thrill of being in on this industry secret was fading away. Even still, those are the most nerve-wracking 180 seconds in the world. This could be your 1,000th flight, and you'd still grip that armrest, tense your shoulders, and whisper a quick prayer under your breath just like everyone else. Because that limbo between flying and landing can feel like an eternity, even though you know it's only 180 seconds. You know it won't last, but sitting there in the middle of it, it feels like it'll never end. It's that middle space, anchored between where you were and where you're going, that feels so uncertain. Even a little shaky.

But then it happens. The wheels meet the pavement, your body slowly unclenches, you turn your phone back on, and you go right back to forgetting that just three minutes ago you were sitting in a chair, 30,000 feet above the Earth. No big deal. Back to scrolling, catching up on the group text, and slipping your shoes back on your feet.

———

I've always wanted to write a book, ever since I was a kid. I'm fascinated by storytelling — a podcast with the perfect sound editing that puts you right in that exact moment, a TV show that tells the story out of order (like *Lost*, minus that bizarre finale), or a movie that subtly hints at the huge twist ending. I wanted to create my own piece of storytelling, but I never had a clue what I would write about. And then—one single day literally changed the entire course of my life, and I thought, *hey, there's a story.*

I woke up happily one morning next to my husband, and was googling divorce lawyers and pregnancy apps by dinner time. And that's when I started counting. 180 seconds. *I'll be back on the ground in no time,* I said to myself. I folded up my marriage like it was a tray table, I buckled my seatbelt around my growing belly, and I counted.

One Mississippi, two Mississippi, three Mississippi ...

When I'm back on solid ground, *then* I can unclench. *Then* I can write it all down.

Well, spoiler alert, I should count slower, because I'm still hanging out in 3B, buddying up to the flight attendants for some extra cookies, because *folks, we're gonna be here awhile.* (Please read that in your best gargled, pilot radio voice.) I've been suspended between flying and landing for quite some time now, waiting for that magical moment when my wheels touch back down. When the flight has come full circle: the leaving, the limbo, and the landing.

But for awhile there, it was still early. I was navigating uncharted waters for several years, and I didn't feel grounded to start writing about anything yet. I was still counting my seconds one afternoon as I listened to a podcast interview with a woman who was struggling with infertility, and something she said lit a spark in me: "Everyone shares the story on the other end, with the happy ending. Not enough people share in the middle of it, and prove that it's okay to be sad *and* joyful at the same time."

I am in the middle of it. And it's lasted a lot longer than I thought it would, but I'm beginning to learn that the nice, soft landing doesn't always come when you think it will. I've been waiting to pull up to the gate for years now, to give me permission to start. But deep into my 180 seconds, I'm finally realizing that the middle can actually be the best place to start. The middle can be the beginning.

As I started from the middle and began writing down my story, I picked up Anne Lamott's book *Bird by Bird*. In it, she quotes E.L. Doctorow, saying that "'writing is like driving a car at night. You can only see as far as your headlights, but you can make the whole trip that way.' You don't have to see where you're going, you don't have to see your destination or everything you will pass along the way. You just have to see two or three feet ahead of you."

My life fell apart in a single day, as you'll read, and I could only see two or three feet in front of me. Even now, four years later as I write this introduction, I still can only see a few feet ahead. Right down to the writing of this book — a friend asked me the other day, *where are you going to end it?* But I can only see as far as my headlights will shine, so I didn't have an answer. I'll know when I get there, I suppose.

After listening to that rogue podcast episode, and feeling the urge to journal more than usual, I felt the tug to talk about the struggles from the middle. So, I decided to take steps. I started writing.

———

I was (and still am) so *very* in the middle, that I have literally written down my life into this manuscript as it happens, and what I am learning from it. Similar lessons keep showing up like a pattern, and this book has quickly developed into something I am truly proud to share with you. A little terrified, but mostly proud.

I'm telling the story I wish I could have read when I was sitting in an attorney's office with a baby in my belly. I'm telling the story I wish I could have read when I was sitting in a birthing class hoping nobody asked where my husband was. I'm telling the story I heard second-hand from friends about "this woman I know who is also pregnant and single." I'm telling the story I've been hearing from countless women online and in my community who say "I'm in the middle, too."

It's a story that I feel at the center of, but that I know is not just my own to tell. I've changed some names to respect privacy, and I want to be very clear that I am not the victim of this story, and there is no villain. If you didn't already know it, writing down your story is therapeutic. It's healing, and even eye-opening to say what happened, how it made you feel, and how you got through it. That's what this book is.

To quote Ms. Lamott again, "We write to expose the unexposed. If there is one door in the castle you have been told not to go through, you must. Otherwise, you'll just be rearranging furniture in rooms you've already been in."

I'm tired of rearranging furniture in my castle, and I'm ready to swing open those doors and face the skeletons and moth balls. And in sharing my own castle closet, it might help another woman who is still rearranging her own furniture.

Because sadly, there's a woman planning her wedding right now who will one day sit at her kitchen table and hear the word *divorce*. And she's going to feel like no one understands what it's like to see her marriage slip through her fingers in an instant. Maybe that woman will read this book, and maybe she will feel a little less alone.

And maybe there's a woman who just read a positive pregnancy test with her partner this week, but next month or next year that partner will walk away, and she'll be unexpectedly thrust into single motherhood, in the middle of figuring out how to be a mother in the first place. Maybe that woman will read this book and feel a little less alone.

And there are men and women of all walks of life, going through all kinds of struggles and seasons of change, and maybe they'll need to read about someone else's mess. Maybe they will read this book and feel a little less alone.

But before I wrote anything for them, I wrote all of this for me.

As my BFF Anne would say (I've quoted her three times now, so we can be BFF's right?!), it was my shitty first draft. *Sorry, Grandma.* Writing is therapy way before writing is income. I wrote this book for me, and I edited it for you. Not for my business or my brand or to advance anything except my own healing, and hopefully someone else's, too.

―――――

One thing you should know about me is that I have a thing with dates. No, not romantic dinner dates. (But those are nice, too, I hear.) I'm talking about calendar dates. Dates that roll around year after year, and remind you of something or someone. Dates that were once just random numbers strung together, but now hold entirely new meaning. Dates you'll never forget, and dates you wish you didn't remember so well. Dates that make you cringe, and dates that make you smile.

July 5, 2014: The date my brother invited me to move to Nashville, Tennessee with him and his family.

July 15, 2015: The date I moved to Nashville, Tennessee.

December 8, 2015: The date I fell in love with someone.

January 18, 2016: The date I was forced out of love with someone.

March 17, 2016: The date I fell in love with a house.

May 29, 2016: The date I moved into that house, which was not in Nashville, Tennessee.

Or, take these, for example ...

October 21, 2013: The date my husband left.

October 21, 2013: The date I found out I was pregnant with our child.

October 21, 2014: The randomly assigned court date to finalize my divorce.

October 21, 2015: The date I started my first relationship after that divorce.

October 21, 2018: The date I released this book you're holding.

Now, *that's* a date to remember, can I get an amen? To add to the irony, I even read the other day that Thomas Edison invented the light bulb on — you guessed it — October 21st.

That light bulb date seems to be my kryptonite, and every year, it rolls around again. And once more, I recall the last few times it rolled around — how different my life looked on those October 21sts. Will something significant happen today? What will all of this look like next October 21st?

The thing about dates is, they're concrete. They're fact, not opinion. They have an order, they are consistent, they literally never change from year to year. There will always be 30 days in September. Like, always.

I like that predictability. Because the other thing about dates is that they are completely *un*predictable. Case in point: October 21st.

But even when the dates carry painful memories, there's something almost comforting in knowing we have something to hold on to that won't waver. We have these markers in time to prove that we're still making our way towards a safe landing. Milestones that remind us to keep moving forward, to make our way through that middle part, however long it may take.

———

To write in the middle of my mess means that I'm writing through my grief, my anger, my bitterness, my resentment. These are real emotions that I haven't overcome. They creep in on the regular, and I'm still learning what to do with them all.

Grief and bitterness: those can be the hardest to grapple with. Just when I think I've made progress, something triggers those two back up to the surface. If this was like any other book where the author shares their story after the dust has settled and they've stuck the landing, this would be the part where they share their redemption. This would be the part where they say they struggled with the mess in the middle, and now they've moved on. They've forgiven and forgotten, the 180 seconds are long gone.

This is not one of those books, and I'm not one of those writers. I haven't forgiven and forgotten yet — I'm working on it, but not there yet. Brené Brown wrote about forgiveness in her incredible book *Rising Strong*, which you'll hear mentioned more than once in this book. In her words, forgiveness means that "something has to die." That sounds morbid and like maybe this book will be a murder mystery novel, but track with me and Brené, here. She explains: "Sometimes we have to kill off and bury being right in order for forgiveness to happen." And in the middle of my mess, I haven't gotten to this place Brené describes just yet. Maybe that will be my next book. *Foreshadowing?*

You may be reading this book because you're sitting in the middle of your own mess, still sorting through emotions and trying to figure out what to do next. You can only see as far as your headlights will reach. You're only halfway through your 180 seconds, and you're scared. If you take one thing away from this book, let it be this: I'm sitting in your mess with you. As I type these words on a screen, I'm four years, one month, and 11 days out from the official inauguration of *my* big mess — and most days, I'm still sitting in it, clenching my armrests with white knuckles. The feelings are still there, and the pain still stings. The bitterness still burrows way down in there and makes itself at home. And it does not make very good company. I was wronged, and I'm still working to bury being right.

————

The other night my ex-husband dropped off our daughter like usual, and we stood in my living room having perhaps one of the most honest conversations we've ever had about what happened four years, one month, and 11 days ago. He apologized for the decisions he made in those early days, and how much it hurt me. He acknowledged that now having an 8-week-old baby with his new wife has opened his eyes to what I actually went through in caring for a newborn by myself. He spoke of the respect he had for me, and I thanked him for validating that that season was HARD. And that most seasons still are, doing this job alone. We spoke of how amazing our daughter is, and how we can't believe we get to be her parents. We spoke of that day, October 21st, and how he remembers the look on my face like it was yesterday. It feels like yesterday to me, too, I agreed. We spoke of the strange reality that we don't really know each other anymore, yet were once husband and wife, and how weird it is to say that to the other person out loud.

Throughout this book, we'll unpack all of that baggage I just dumped in one paragraph, but the last thing we talked about that evening was something that I had been terrified to bring up with him — this book. I knew I would need to tell him that I was starting the process of writing it, but I was waiting for the right time. And maybe procrastinating a little bit, because this conversation was not going to come easily. But then the hatch opened up, and I started my 180 seconds, praying I'd stick the landing. I acknowledged that this story is just as much his as it is mine. And it's part of Poppy's story, and part of Melany's story, and even part of that 8-week-old baby's story. (If you're thinking, *hold up, Kelsey, who are all these people,* we'll get to all that.) There are a lot of characters in this weird narrative we've created for ourselves — and in writing this book, I am acutely aware of all of them.

I didn't know what his reaction would be, but I was pleasantly surprised. Graciously, he gave me his blessing for this project, saying I had never given him any reason not to trust me in sharing our story in an honest, respectful way. Any time I've told a friend or family member that I'm writing this book, they always shower me with encouragement and support, of which I am extremely grateful. But I realized today, having this most honest conversation with him, that his opinion was actually the one I cared the most about. His approval was, oddly enough, the one I was waiting for.

I know eyes from all sides will read this book, and I expect even my daughter will read it someday, too. It includes the story of her parents, but it's so much more than that. It's the story of her first years, her mother's hardest years, and how she taught me to just *be better*. It's a story that proves our resilience as mothers and daughters. A story that weaves silver linings into even the most heartbreaking seasons of this wild life we all get to live. It's the story of my 180 seconds, the limbo that hasn't quite turned into a landing just yet. A story that I hope you can spot yourself in, somewhere between these pages.

It's a tricky task, as the teller of this intricate, winding story, but it's an important one — because this is a worthy story to share.

CHAPTER ONE

THE DIVORCE

At rock bottom, you thought you'd never move on. But now you saw it all with new eyes. You looked in the mirror again and saw you weren't the person you thought you were: you were someone even better, someone more independent. Someone who stood their ground despite all the changes swirling all around them. You didn't just move forward. You found your way back to yourself.

SHANNON MOIRA

F our years ago on this exact date and at this exact time, I saw his mouth form the word *divorce,* but I couldn't quite hear the sound. It all went quiet, like in a movie when you see the character still talking, but the voice is drowned out with music or just silence. It was like that. He continued talking and explaining and apologizing, but I couldn't hear anything.

Today, October 21, 2017, I'm sitting in a pew, in an old church. A beautiful lace backdrop sets the stage up front, and a bride, my friend Ana, walks down the aisle toward her beaming, sweating groom. The irony of this exact moment is not lost on me: that the exact same day — the same event, even — can have such profoundly different meanings in two different stories.

They say vows to one another. They exchange rings. They serve each other communion. The pastor talks about each of these symbols, and what they represent for the longevity of the marriage that is starting today.

I can't help but remember my own wedding day — we exchanged those same three things: the vows, the rings, the communion. I remember standing before my own groom, reciting the words. Beaming and sweating. We were 21, and we claimed to know what we were signing up for.

But it hits me now, sitting in this pew, watching these motions play out as a spectator. Those three symbols are just that — symbols. Man-made representations of something we can't quite comprehend. A bond we know is so powerful and so precious, that we have to give it something our minds can wrap around.

A ring, that'll do. A ring made from a precious metal, a perfect circle that can't be broken. But a ring can be slipped on and off. A ring can be tucked inside a drawer when things get hard. A ring can be sold back to the jeweler for $120 after the divorce papers are signed.

Okay, we'll do communion. The first act together as husband and wife. We'll serve each other, as we remember our Creator who brought us together. This act is genuine on a wedding day, in that dress and that tux. But on a Monday, we'll realize so much of what went on between then and now was just that — an act. One person serving, the other acting.

Fine then, a vow. We'll proclaim our love and devotion in front of all of these people. They'll be our witnesses, they'll hold us accountable. But vows are just words. Vows are easily forgotten. And then vows can be

The beginning is perhaps more difficult than anything else, but take heart, it will all turn out alright.

VINCENT VAN GOGH

suddenly remembered when you're sitting across the kitchen table from a partner who is asking for a way out.

But the witnesses? Surely they can weigh in. Of course they will, but at the end of the day, they can only cover their mouths as they read an email from left field that their friends couldn't make it last. The jig is up.

So we're nearing the end of the ceremony, and I'm left wondering — how can a marriage stay together if all our man-made symbols don't stick? Don't get me wrong: of course I'm well aware that a ring and a vow and a crowd of people aren't the things that hold a marriage together. But when you're sitting in a pew, knowing all the hours of work that went into making this exact moment happen, you can't help but feel the presence these symbols carry. Even my cynical, divorced self felt it.

Ana and her groom finish their rituals, they turn to face us, their witnesses, and they're announced as a new man and a new wife. We all beam proudly as if we've done something besides sit in a pew, and I whisper under my breath, *God, when all these symbols fade away, and they realize it's just their daily decision to keep this whole party going, may they make the right choice. Don't let them end up like us.*

Now, where's the reception, and is there an open bar?

We met in the youth group, and I had a crush on his best friend. I hardly noticed him, but his best friend was tall, mysterious, and had a small, side smile that made you smile back as a reflex. And then I learned that Side Smile also had a girlfriend. A girlfriend of many, many years — as many as you can have as a sophomore in high school — and they were like *this*… (you can't see me, but I'm crossing my fingers). So then I noticed Side Smile's sidekick, Dustin, the one I would marry five years later. The one with the lip ring and the tattoos. *What sophomore in high school has tattoos?* This one did. He had long, greasy hair, baggy pants, a beard, for goodness' sake. And I thought for sure I could fix him.

Behind the bad boy exterior, Dustin was actually quite gentle and lighthearted. And behind the gentle lightheartedness, he had a vastly different home life than I did. His family was extremely impoverished. He grew up with nearly-bare cupboards, and less than ideal role models. Actually, zero role models. Until he was in high school, started going to church, and ran into me at a youth lock-in on New Year's Eve.

We started dating after several months of making googly eyes, and all those other awkward things you do as a teenager to see if a boy likes you back. He didn't have a car, so I drove. He didn't have a job, so I paid. And thus we laid the unhealthy foundation for a relationship that would carry us both through the next decade.

Dustin asked me to marry him the day after he was supposed to. He had planned to ask me on a walk through the Nature Center, one of our favorite places to go. We would walk for hours, talk for hours.

We were just barely not teenagers, and it was free. He took me back there one evening in June, and I knew that morning that that would be the day he would ask me to marry him. We walked down the dirt path, and at every turn I thought, *is this it? Is this where he stops me, and bends his knee?*

Then we came to a clearing, and it happened. No, he didn't ask me to marry him. We ran into a big neon sign that read *Trail Closed*. It was flooded from the heavy rain that week. We were instructed to turn back and go out the way we came in.

Looking back, this moment is so ironic, it hurts. But at the time, I was upset. I was pissed. My proposal was supposed to happen down that trail. That's where we were supposed to start our lives. But we were met with a literal roadblock, telling us to turn back. Don't go this way. Had I lived more life than just a starry-eyed, naive, 20-year-old, maybe I would have taken the hint.

So we turned around, walked back through the trail in silence, back to my car. We drove home with no words, both of us frustrated by the moment we both knew was missed.

The next day, I was in my apartment, taking a nap, and was startled awake. Dustin touched my arm, and I opened my eyes to see him sitting there with a ring box. I can't tell you what he said to me in that moment because I honestly don't remember. You know those first few moments when you wake up from a deep sleep? You're not quite sure what day it is, what time it is, what happened before you fell asleep, and what you should be doing now. My memory from this moment is literally a talking head, moving lips, but no sound. I missed my own proposal, yet here I was saying *yes*, watching a ring slipped onto my finger, and shoving down the twinge of doubt that

In writing down this part of my story, I can't *not* see the similarities. Thinking pieces of your life would play out this certain way, and then startling awake to a different story. A different ending.

was trying to surface. *Is this the right time? Is he the right person? Is this how it was all supposed to happen?*

In writing down this part of my story — and knowing what the next five years would hold — I can't not see the similarities. Thinking pieces of your life would play out this certain way, and then startling awake to a different story. A different ending. It's frustrating. *What did you miss, Kelsey? Why was your head in the sand? Why did you say yes and put on the ring?* I know the answer to those types of questions now.

––––––––

During our engagement, I went to Scotland for a study abroad program. It was a life-changing four months for me. I was opened up to a myriad of cultures and lifestyles that were so different than what I had been exposed to in middle America. I discovered my love for traveling alone, marching to my own drum, and the neon-orange beverage of choice for Scots — Irn Bru. I crossed paths with other students for this short, formative season in all of our lives — when we were discovering ourselves and exploring our beliefs. And then we all went back home. Back to Connecticut, and Minnesota, and Philly. Back to Germany, and back to Palestine.

Dustin and I, we were engaged to each other during those four months, but we weren't *engaged* with each other. We weren't on the same wavelength. I was living abroad, turning down dinner invitations to stay in and finish a freelance project for an extra $200 that we could stock away in our savings account. He was getting another tattoo. I'd be lying if I didn't say it was frustrating. Once again, I was driving us, I was paying for us. I was taking care of us. And it would take me many years to realize how badly I wanted someone else to take care of me.

I came home from Scotland with four months to spare before our May wedding. I moved in with my mom to save money, I handmade every inch of that wedding on a shoestring, and we professed our love in front of close friends and family, blue skies above, and dusk settling into the trees around us. It was a Sunday — May 17, 2009. We were truly happy, I believe, and there was no turning back on the trail.

The first few years of marriage were like anyone else's — learning to live with another human, constantly comparing expectations with our reality. We moved to a new apartment, then we bought a house, then we got a dog. We followed all the steps laid out by the friends and families building lives in tandem with ours. We were trying to be happy, but in retrospect, I can see the disconnect underneath the surface. My doubts would occasionally creep back in, finding holes in my perfect plan, and oozing out slowly like honey — except unsweet. *Did I settle? Should we have waited? Were we too young? Is this right?*

But you're married, and you're 25, and you know everything.

It was October 21, 2013, a Monday. Sitting in my office at the design agency I worked at, my phone dings with a text message:

When you get home, can we talk about something?

Usually a text like this would get my heart racing, and my mind reeling. Even just typing that on a screen is doing the job, right now. But for some reason, reading that on my phone that afternoon, I didn't feel anything. He must have a new hobby he wants to try. Or maybe an idea for his new business we're starting up. Maybe he wants to go vegetarian again. Dear God, please don't let it be that; I can't do any more tofu.

I packed up and drove home through leaves falling, and distinctly remember feeling noticeably happy.

———

A few minutes later, the unraveling began. I saw his mouth form the word *divorce,* but I couldn't quite hear the sound. It all went quiet, like in a movie when you see the character still talking, but their voice is drowned out with music or just silence. It was like that. He kept talking and explaining and apologizing, but I couldn't hear anything.

We were sitting at the kitchen table, overlooking our backyard in the house we had bought two years prior. The dog we rescued around the same time, Cooper, was chasing squirrels, and I watched him prance, pounce, and sneak up on one after another after another. He'd put his paws up on the big maple tree in the middle of our yard, barking up at the squirrels, as if they might just run back down the trunk of the tree and right into his mouth. But they were just barely out of his reach.

Slowly, I turned back to the voice next to me and it became clearer, less muffled, and I made out some words:

I just don't want to be married anymore. I don't want the house, I don't want the dog, I don't want the business, and I don't even think I want kids. I don't know what life I do want, but I just know it's not this.

Shock doesn't really describe what was going through my brain.

Picture this: A pitcher throwing a banana to the plate, the batter swinging to hit it head-on, the banana shattering into a million strands of spaghetti, the noodles falling back towards the field, then the grass oozing up with alfredo, each base turning into a plate, and each player pulling forks out of their back pockets to catch the spaghetti and swirl it around in the alfredo — *that* would have seemed more normal to me than this conversation I was having with my husband at our kitchen table. And good Lord, I'm hungry.

I was still holding my bag from work over my shoulder. He was waiting for my response, but I didn't have one. I was clutching that bag, hoping if I squeezed hard enough it could rewind me back to the office, and I could just stay there forever and not walk into this bizarre conversation.

But I was stuck. Literally stuck sitting at this table, watching my dog play outside, unable to move or breathe or have much of a coherent thought about this whole thing. A sudden stranger staring at me, waiting for a reply.

But I was a different kind of stuck, too. I was stuck between two emotions that I couldn't quite wrap my head around.

I felt instant relief.

And I felt instant guilt for feeling instant relief.

When the husband says *divorce*, here's what your brain *should* be saying:

Okay Eyes, cue the tears.

Heart, beat triple-time please.

Voice, beg him to stay — ya know, movie stuff.

And Body, keel over with grief. Readyyyy, go!

But this moment was different. You never expect to have this conversation with your husband, but if you see it play out in a movie or between Ross and Rachel, you have *kind of* an idea of how you'd respond, right? Please agree with me, because I want you to know how unexpected this was — both that we were having this conversation, and my immediate reaction to it.

I don't know what life I do want, but I just know it's not this.

To add to my confusion, here's what I clearly felt God say to me in the lull after Dustin's less-than-helpful explanation: *You've served your time in this, you're done. You can go now. I have better things for you than this.*

Dramatic screech of the record here for a sec, because I need to tell you something else. I have never felt God speak to me in any clear, that-was-for-sure-not-me kind of way. Like never ever, *ever*. In fact, I'm usually the skeptic sitting in the back row, arms crossed, rolling my eyes when someone says they heard something from God. I don't like admitting that, but it's true.

Oh, thank God. I literally felt this in my gut. *Oh, thank God. This is my ticket out.*

And that's when I knew that my heart wasn't in this marriage any more than his was, I just hadn't realized it yet.

The room was still silent, and he was still waiting. He looked like a puppy who had just been caught smearing his crap all over a new rug. He kind of *was* a puppy who had just been caught smearing his crap across my new rug. He looked embarrassed, guilty, and scared.

"I want the house," I heard myself say.

Kelsey, what are you saying? Beg him to stay! Save the marriage!

"Of course. You can have literally whatever you want," he replied.

"And the dog, and the car we just bought," I continued.

Helloooo, this is not how you respond to The Divorce Talk, you idiot.

"Absolutely," he nodded.

Ok, then.

We sat in silence for a few more minutes, then he mumbled something about going to stay at his mom's house for the night, and time apart blah blah blah, the muffled talk was kicking back in, and I was tuning it out.

I stayed there at the table, bag in hand, all the way until he closed the door behind him, and I heard the garage door go back down. These were the handful of minutes when I thought my only problem was that pesky divorce.

It wasn't until moments later when I actually cried for the first time, staring at the freshly-peed-on pregnancy test. The blue plus sign staring back at me, clear as day, screaming, *but wait, there's more!*

And I thought for sure someone was playing a joke on me.

I know what you're thinking: *why take a pregnancy test right after your husband asks for a divorce?* And to that I say, *well why the heck not?! Could be fun.* Ok, maybe not so fun. The truth is, we had

I'm so mad at him. He pulled the rug out from under me, and left me to fend for myself. He left his pregnant wife to take care of his house, his dog, his bills, his responsibilities. I wish he would grow up. He said he wants to so badly, so why won't he? What's stopping him? Why is he throwing all of this away?

In the months after the divorce, I cycled through the stages of grief, and got stuck real good on the Anger stage. I was livid one evening, and felt the sudden urge to write. That was maybe one of the first times I wrote as pure therapy. I was sitting in my living room, no paper in arm's reach, so I grabbed an old planner from the bookshelf next to me, turned to an empty week, and feverishly wrote down every thought that came to mind. I covered that weekly spread in angry rants, pleas to God, and some really great digs that I'd love to share, but I will refrain. I spilled everything into that old planner, then sat back in relief. I felt lighter. The pain felt a little further away.

Many years later, as I was writing this very book, I would watch a show called *The Marvelous Mrs. Maisel* about a woman whose husband leaves her out of the blue. Something she says in one particular scene would perfectly describe this anger I felt burning so hot inside of me that day in my living room with my outdated planner: "You said you didn't want this life, but this *is* your life. You didn't go anywhere exotic or different, you just went across the street."

been trying for nearly a year. I had a stash of pregnancy tests in the cabinet right across from the toilet where I was headed to have my after-work pee, before I was so rudely interrupted with that whole divorce thing. But I really couldn't tell you what exactly prompted me to take the test when I finally sat down on the throne. I just took my seat, stared at the cabinet across from me, and thought, *Huh. Well that would change things.*

––––––––

When your entire life changes literally overnight, it can be a hard thing to explain quickly to a stranger, without feeling like you're dumping a heaping load of dirty laundry on them. A bank teller, for example, to whom you're trying to tactfully explain why you're closing all your bank accounts, and opening all new ones — without crying. It is a feat. I succeeded in the explaining, I did not in the not-crying.

Karen The Kind Bank Teller would end up calling me in the weeks to come, just to check on me, asking if I needed anything. She personally mailed me folded up receipts when my paycheck got switched over to the new account. She sent a handwritten note at Christmas encouraging me to stay strong during the holidays. She reached across her desk, squeezed my hand, and told me she was divorced too, when I said the D word for the first time out loud. Sweet, Karen. And I had only dumped half of my dirty laundry on her desk: she didn't even know about the baby.

The Baby. Holy crap, I'm having a baby.

In any other season of this weird show called My Life, this would have been just an everyday trip to the bank. But even the littlest errands take big courage when you wake up one day and you're relearning how to do everything with these two new facts about yourself — you're getting a divorce and you're pregnant. And neither of which anyone is ever truly prepared for.

You go to the grocery store, run to Target, out to grab a pizza (cause ain't no way you're doing dishes right now), and you feel like you're wearing a sandwich board that spills all the contents of the last two weeks of your life. Surely all these nice Target shoppers know.

They didn't know. And I didn't know that this was the easiest season to keep my secrets to myself — no belly, no problem. When I started sporting the full-size basketball under my clothes was when the most annoying comment came out: *Oh, you and your husband must be so excited!*

I just nod with my fake smile, do the ol' hand on the belly motion, and excuse myself to the frozen aisle for more ice cream. *You don't know the half of it, grocery store lady.*

I have this weird memory association with food. Certain dishes take me straight back to a very specific moment, and every time I eat that dish, I can't shake that memory. It all started when I was a kid, maybe kindergarten-ish. Me and my brothers and my parents were sitting around the dinner table, when my dad spotted a huge black snake circling its way up our porch railing, heading straight for a birdhouse. Our house backed up to a big open field, so these big black snakes (that's the official term), would occasionally slither their way in and torture my poor mother and her bird houses. My dad jumped

up from the table, and ran out the
back door. He grabbed a shovel, and
he was on a mission. We all stood up
a little from our chairs and watched
him as he beat the big black snake
down off the railing and bashed its
head into the end of the shovel, blood pouring out everywhere. He
dumped the snake over the fence into the field, came back up into
the house, and washed the blood off his hands.

> The Lord helps
> the fallen and lifts
> those bent beneath
> their loads.
>
> PSALM 145:14

No one said a word as we all slowly sat back down, pulled our
chairs back up the table, and attempted to finish our spaghetti. Or at
least push it around our plates until Mom said we could be done.

I couldn't eat spaghetti for weeks after that. And even when I
could again, spaghetti would always be associated with that bloody
mid-dinner snake scene.

Fast forward about 20 years, and I found myself sitting at my
kitchen table, at home during my lunch break, eating a plate of spaghetti, thinking about the black snake. Every few minutes I'd half
turn my head around to see the progress behind me. I'd quickly turn
back around if he noticed me. You could cut the tension in the air
with a knife, that afternoon. Or a shovel, perhaps.

It had been about 2 weeks since my life had exploded, and
Dustin was moving out. Packing up just a handful of things from
our house — from our near 10 year stint together — and leaving.

I should have gone out for lunch, I thought with every bite.

It was the world's longest lunch break, and I shoveled spaghetti
into my mouth (no pun intended), pretending it was a totally normal

day. My husband is moving out today, and I'm sitting here watching it happen. Totally normal.

I left while he was still packing up his things. *Do I holler good-bye to him from the kitchen? Do I ask him to lock up when he leaves? Of course he'll lock up, he lives here. I mean ... he used to live here. This is weird.*

I snuck out quietly, and once outside in the fresh, tensionless air, finally took a breath.

I'll never forget the garage door slowly creaking up after I came home from work later that day. The reality was settling in. His bikes were gone. He was an avid cyclist, and so our garage was always littered with bikes and gear and bike gear. (I don't know anything about bikes, okay?) I sat there in my running car, staring at the empty garage for a good 10 minutes.

Now it's real. Now he's really gone.

I walked slowly through the house, and took inventory of the holes — or lack thereof. He took his clothes, his toiletries, his collection of hobbies long forgotten, an HDMI cable he felt particularly attached to, and that was it. It was surreal. I finished my tour in the spare bedroom, what was his office at the time, and finally let my work bag slide off my shoulder. Once again, I clung to it hoping it would take this weird mess away. I fell to my knees in the middle of that room, and felt the full wave of emotion pour over my body. The wave that was waiting to crash down over the last two weeks. The wave that was hovering just at the curve, enveloping me almost completely, but not yet touching me. Like those pictures of surfers you see riding through a tunnel of water, and you wonder who the heck is holding the camera.

MY TOP 5 FOOD ASSOCIATIONS

1. Tootsie Rolls + back surgery. My eyes were bigger than my stomach, as I was recovering from spinal fusion surgery when I was 14, special thanks to scoliosis. Morphine and fake chocolate don't mix, and after eating an entire bag, I puked up every roll.

2. Stouffer's microwave lasagna + my dad. My dad almost always has a Stouffer's microwave lasagna in his freezer. Like always. The taste of those slightly artificial tomatoes and little nuggets of cheese product transports me straight back to his couch gushing over Paige's pixie cut on Trading Spaces.

3. Snow Caps + movie theaters. The movie candy that Dustin always knew I loved. I don't really eat Snow Caps anymore, I go for popcorn. Or fried pickles, because that tastes like Nashville.

4. Starbucks Chai Lattes + crying. Speaking of Nashville, this was my order every Thursday night after counseling. That spicy taste takes me right back to sitting in my car in the Starbucks parking lot off Old Hickory Boulevard. I'm certain the barista knew me as The Girl Who Was Obviously Just Crying.

5. Blackberries + my grandmother. I grew up picking these hand-staining berries in my grandmother's backyard. She dug up that plant and took it with her from house to house, and it grew stronger and healthier with each new beginning. Fresh soil, fresh start. My house today is the same age as her — 86 years young — and a blackberry bush has been cycling through seasons on the southwest corner as long as I've lived here.

The wave was waiting to crash, and it finally did on the floor of that bedroom that would soon become a nursery. The room that would be painted minty green on a *Bachelor* Monday night a few months later. The room where, a few months after that, my dad and I would nearly lose our religion, I tell you, trying to find the right ceiling wires to install a fan for my summer due date. The room where I would find myself many, many times that summer, face down on the arena floor, as the lovely Brenè Brown puts it, begging my baby to go to sleep.

The waves would crash over and over again in that room, as I watched my weird new life unfold like scenes from a movie. *A lot went down in here,* I would say to myself another year later, standing in that empty room the day I moved out.

The waves continue to crash, even today, because that's how grief works. It comes in waves — sometimes you see it coming and you can brace for it. *Looking at you, holiday season.* And other times it comes out of nowhere and knocks you down — pulls you under into the swirling sand and shells and you don't know which way is up. *Looking at you, random Saturday morning yoga class.* But you find the surface every time. Your head comes back up for air, you wipe the salt from your eyes as you find your bearings again, and you can see everyone around you still carrying on, splashing in

> Grief comes in waves — sometimes you see it coming and you can brace for it. And other times it comes out of nowhere. It knocks you down, pulls you under into the swirling sand and shells, and you don't know which way is up.

the water. And you remember, *yes, this is living! I'm fine! This is fun! We're all fine! Are we all fine?*

We're not all fine. But yes, that's still living.

————

The next wave of grief came when I was sitting alone in an attorney's office for the very first time, telling the man across the desk the events of the last two weeks. Even he, a divorce attorney, was dumbfounded. *Yes sir, it appears that is my life right now. So how do I make it official?*

He talked through options while I held back first trimester nausea, and we finally decided to just sit on it. In the state of Missouri, a divorce case with a pregnant wife can't be finalized until the child is born. Apparently Social Security numbers and birth dates are important to have in legal documents — who knew? I didn't even know the gender of said child yet, so I had to just sit on it. My egg, and my forthcoming divorce. Until it hatched.

And so we waited. Later that year, I would carry my sleeping three week old baby back into that office, and quietly sign papers to finally start the divorce process.

A wave of grief swept over me every time I walked into that office, and after a couple months of back and forth negotiations, we were both ready to sign it all away. Only one step left: appear together before a judge, and officially dissolve our marriage.

Dissolve is a funny word. It makes it sound like it was never there. Like we were never there, together. It breaks it down into such tiny particles, that you can't even see it anymore. But you *can* see it. When you dissolve salt into a cup of water, there's those few moments in the beginning when it's all murky and swirling. It's chaotic in there, everything is moving so fast. You think, *no way this is going to work, it's all right there. I can still see it!* And then, kind of suddenly, it all just … fizzles away. Dissolves. The water settles back down, and it's clear. It's still, and it's calm. And you're like, *huh, look at that. Everything's fine.*

But take a drink, and you can taste the salt. The bitterness, the anger, the grief, it's all still there. It's just broken down into the tiniest of particles making it harder to spot. But on the flip side — and rather unfortunately so — it also makes it easier to hide.

I opened up the letter after work one day, and laughed out loud. Our randomly assigned court date was October 21, 2014. A year to the date after he dumped a whole salt shaker into my water, the swirling would finally be dissolved, and the water could start to clear.

CHAPTER TWO

THE PReGNANCY

If you can stand the open space in your life for just a little bit of time,
it can be the precursor to the greatest blessings you have ever seen.

ALLISON FALLON

That night of The Divorce Talk and the pregnancy test, I found myself sitting on my mom's couch, and it was a little like the afternoon he proposed marriage to me. Talking heads, words obviously coming out, but no sound. I have no idea what my mom said that night, as her daughter's life was crumbling in real time. I'm sure there was encouragement and solidarity and all the things moms say when you're running to them for help, but unfortunately I don't remember a word. The only thing I remember is our moods leveling out, one of us cracking a joke to break up all the crying, and her saying, "Well, you need to download one of those baby apps on your phone."

Of course. How could I forget the baby apps? I pulled out my phone, found the first one that popped up in the search and downloaded it. I typed in the due date I was roughly calculating in my head, and off it went, planning out the next nine months for me. And then, it appeared.

You are 4 weeks pregnant. Your baby is the size of a poppyseed.

"Poppyseed." I sat back on the couch, and said it aloud to Mom. "The baby is the size of a poppyseed. Holy crap."

We both sat there, trying to wrap our minds around a baby the size of a poppyseed, but of course we couldn't quite get there.

Poppyseed. There is a poppyseed growing into a human, inside of my body.

At some point, I drove home — back up Fremont thinking how cool it would be to fix up an old house on this historic street. But the dreams I had for myself were starting to look a little different now. Fixing up an old house may have been on my radar yesterday — not even that, it could have been 12 hours ago — but that little idea would have to be folded up and tucked neatly into the very back of the junk drawer, because a baby was coming in nine months. Ready or not.

Let's focus on that, Kels. One thing at a time.

I turned off Fremont, drove some more, and pulled into my tiny garage on Stewart. I turned off the car, and sat there for a bit. I ran through the series of events again, wondering if maybe this day — the literal weirdest day of my life — was all a dream. I finally came inside, and curled up in bed with my dog. I sent my mom the Made It Home Text, and she replied with a message I wouldn't soon forget:

"Good night Kels, I love you. And good night, Poppyseed."

———

This story is hard to tell, because you can't have one without the other. *I'm pregnant ... oh yeah, and we're getting a divorce.* Or: *we're getting a divorce ... and oh yeah, I'm pregnant.* Which comes first, the bombshell or the egg?

For the first week or two, no one knew except my mother (and, of course, Dustin). Knowing the weight she would carry, I selfishly asked her to keep this secret for me while we sorted things out. Surely this would just be a phase: he would realize the monumental repercussions, and he would come to his senses. And at first, it appeared like that was happening.

I told Dustin I was pregnant the day after he asked for the divorce. We sat on the edge of our bed after work that evening, and I didn't beat around the bush about it. In fact, I think my mama instincts kicked in almost immediately.

"I'm pregnant, and I need to know now if you're in or you're out," I told him. "I refuse to spend the next nine months in limbo." I told him I would go to counseling with him, if that's what he wanted. I also told him I wasn't afraid to be a single mom. I was even a little surprised to hear it come out of my own mouth. *Was I really not afraid?* Or maybe I just didn't know any different.

I'm not sure if it was the trauma of that whole week literally changing the course of my life, or maybe it was the baby brain, but I really don't remember much about his reaction. But here's what I do remember: he said he was in. But then he acted like he was out.

We cooked dinner together that night, he put his hand on my belly, and we acted like the last 5 minutes of a *Friends* episode when all the storylines start to get resolved. But that was the extent of our episode. The rest of the week, we were like ships passing in the night. We hardly spoke. He didn't come home some evenings, and when he did, he slept on the couch.

I spent the next week pretending like everything was fine. *Everything's fine!* I called out from the waves. I carefully crafted responses and explanations to keep what was actually happening tucked neatly under the surface. Just out of reach. No one would ever suspect this. That's what made pretending easy, but that's what made the truth so hard to tell. Pretending everything was fine was easier than explaining the truth.

The idea that we would try to work things out moved further and further out of reach, and the reality set in that he really wasn't in this, even with a baby on the way. On Halloween, ten days after the bombshell, he finally came back home and we talked. It was for sure over. He had made his decision. Looking back, it's hard for me to reconcile how nonchalant I felt about the whole thing initially.

Divorce is a go? Ok, I'll close the joint bank accounts tomorrow. Although it's a Saturday, so I'll have to get there before noon, and I also need to return those pants because they're definitely not going to fit me now. I'm sorry, what are we talking about?!

The weeks that followed were a blur.

I told my brother Taylor, first. Partially because he happened to call me that Halloween morning for our usual catch-up. But also because I was the last person he called when he came out to all of us two years before — he called us in order of hardest to tell to easiest to tell. I knew he was gay all along. I dumped my dirty laundry on him, over the phone, sitting at the same table where the laundry got so dirty the week before. Taylor offered to let me stay with him in New York, to get out of town for a bit, and I took him up on it a few months later. If there hadn't been a poppyseed growing in my belly, I probably would have moved there. My house was growing darker and feeling stuffier the longer we talked, like the air had been sucked right out, windows slammed shut behind it. It was still Halloween, but not a single trick-or-treater came to my door.

I texted my dad in the Target checkout line the next day, after my mom and I had finished a harrowing session of retail therapy, and asked him if we could talk about something important that after-

That's what made pretending easy, but that's what made the truth so hard to tell. Pretending everything was fine was easier than explaining the truth.

noon. The other shoppers were asking whoever was on the other end of their calls if they needed to pick up more bread, or that they'd found a cute fruit bowl for the kitchen, or what was that sweater you were looking for? While I was nervously figuring out how to tell the person on the other end of *my* call that my marriage had just ended. A few hours later, Dad and I held hands in his driveway as silence fell over us both. We were in old lawn chairs at the opening of his garage, his favorite place to sit and patrol the neighborhood. Such a Dad thing to do. Holding his hand, I was a little girl again. My small, soft fingers enveloped in his big, weathered hands, I felt safe and understood. We both recognized the gravity of this moment, but neither of us quite knew what to say.

I told my best friend Kayla a few days later as she made us tea in her kitchen, and I could tell she already knew what was coming. That's what happens when you've been best friends for the last decade, and entire conversations can be had with just facial expressions and hand motions. We made small talk, dancing around the real reason I was there, while she picked out two mugs, poured hot water over the peppermint tea bags, and steam flushed both our faces. I clutched the tea cup to distract my nervous hands, and told her the truth of the last few weeks.

> Yet God has made
> everything beautiful
> for its own time.
>
> ECCLESIASTES 3:11 (NLT)

She held space for me on her couch that warm afternoon, and we cried together. Grief for the marriage, joy for the baby. Nine months later, she would drive to my house and rub cypress oil on my swollen postpartum feet even when she was already late to church, because that's the kind of friend she is.

In the same week, my mom and I went over to my brother Grant's house. I sat at the table with him and his wife Sheila while my mom entertained my three nieces upstairs. Let's keep their innocence a little longer, shall we? I told Grant and Sheila the tale I had told thrice already, saying *whatever* to the tears this time. The weight of what I had been carrying around for weeks was getting to be too much to bear, and my puffy face and constant messy-bun hair were proof. I had been in the same ratty sweatshirt and leggings for days. I finished my spiel while Sheila kicked Grant under the table, motioning for him to give me a hug, and I searched my sleeve for a clean spot to wipe my nose. He hugged me later, but in the moment all he said were two things that neither of us have ever forgotten: *You're gonna be a kick-ass mom,* and *This is gonna make a crazy story someday.*

After telling my two bosses at work in the weeks that followed — hello, doctor appointments *and* attorney meetings — I was officially done rehashing this story in person. We had a whole melting pot of friends left to tell, but the only thing I knew to do — or had energy for — was to craft an email. I spent hours writing and rewriting it one evening at my coffee table until it felt honest, but not exhaustive. Mutual, but not actually my decision. I sent it to Dustin first, like an awkward shitty first draft to see if he was okay with it. Yeah, I know. Don't say it.

He was gracious about it, like he would be for years to come of awkward encounters, and I quickly learned that for an ex-husband, he was a good one. I've met so many women whose exes are in jail, abusive, controlling, or just make their lives a living hell. I can't imagine being chained to that for the rest of my life, so for a kind ex-husband, I am incredibly thankful. I sent the email off to friends, and spent the next week fielding replies. It was sad, and it was weird, and it was the only way I knew how to tell the people I cared about.

————

Over the next couple months, my belly grew bigger and harder to hide, and I finally had the weird last weight I was dreading for Phase One of my never-ending story: *How do you tell Facebook?*

It is not lost on me, neither then nor now, how ridiculous this sounds. I was perhaps more annoyed by the fact that I had this dumb social media conundrum to face, than the original divorce-and-pregnant conundrum I was in in the first place.

I would stand in line at the grocery store, tactfully crafting ways to share both pieces of news at the same time, typing mock sentences into my phone, and then promptly erasing them. *How stupid is this,* I would think. Then I'd push my loot closer to the cashier: *Yes, these three cartons of ice cream are all for me, thank you.*

A couple weeks before Christmas, I finally landed on a draft that felt honest without being hurtful, the bitter with the sweet. I kept it fairly vague and hoped the sudden deletion of any photo with Dustin in it would be a big enough hint. I hit Post, felt really silly about it all, and then watched my village rise up around me.

> *December 13, 2013*
> *These last couple months have been some of the most difficult in my life, and included some of the toughest decisions I hope I ever have to face. But a bittersweet surprise has emerged in the form of a little baby that will be joining my life at the end of June. Though this pregnancy has not been at all what I would have imagined, I am beyond thrilled to see what the future holds for me and my little one. Thank you SO much to my incredible family and friends who have shown me nothing but love, support, and encouragement. Your kindness during this difficult season has meant the world to me.*

I share what I wrote in that post, here, because sometime in 2015 I got an email from a woman named Jennifer who found herself in the early stages of divorce, and was struggling with the same weird question I had about how to tell your friends. I felt honored that she reached out to me and trusted me — a stranger on the Internet

— with this piece of her life that she had hardly shared with anyone yet. We talked on Skype, we talked again on the phone, and I started to see the Lord working out all things for good. There's the great line from a writer I love, Hannah Brencher, that says, "One day you'll be out of this. And all the things you felt — all the places you went in the dark — will help someone come out of the woods, too."

The comments and messages flooded in, and their encouragement and support overwhelmed me to tears — still do. I don't know what I was expecting, but the kindness that people showed to me during this season of my life completely humbled me to no avail. It felt embarrassing to have to share with all those friends — those witnesses to our marriage — that we had failed. We were undoing it all. It got too hard. But their unconditional love and support showed me that better days were ahead. This was part of a much bigger story, and it would all kick off like a marathon with that baby — that Poppyseed.

———

My sister-in-law, Sheila, came with me to my first doctor's appointment, and we laughed about how every person in the waiting room for sure thought I was a teen mom. I think I cried at almost every doctor's appointment after that — half from the weird emotions, half from the hormones. And having her there (veteran mom of three) to help break it all in — well, it meant the world to me.

My brother, Taylor, flew in from New York for Thanksgiving that year — the first time ever, and the only time since. I was about a month into this whole mess, and for him to make the extra trip to be here for my first holiday is something I will always treasure. We didn't tell my mom until he showed up on her door, and she legit almost peed her pants. It was THE BEST.

On Valentine's Day I got the heck outta Dodge, stayed off Facebook, and flew to California to see my fellow single ladies, Anna and Adie. We laughed til we cried on cheesy Hollywood Stars tours, waited in line for way too long at a new gourmet hot dog restaurant in LA (which we found fitting for a bunch of single ladies on Valentine's Day), ate the most amazing Sidecar donuts every morning, and drew our names in the sand at the beach. It was the absolute perfect distraction.

For my birthday in March, I went to New York to see Taylor. He arranged tea service for us at The Plaza, he ordered me fancy mocktails at every bar, and we did a 7-course pasta tasting that literally changed my life. If you can't tell, I was in my second trimester, and eating all the things. I looked like a swollen, tired whale in every photo, but I l-o-v-e-d this trip.

My other brother, Grant, kept me laughing. He'll be the first to tell you, consoling isn't his strength. But I'll be the first to tell you that he made me laugh more in those nine months than anyone. It helped me forget all this craziness for just a few seconds, even his never-ending fat jokes. Our long-running, not-sure-how-it-even-started joke de jour was finally very applicable to my growing belly. Strangers would get wide-eyed when he'd holler at a restaurant, "Fatty, need more fries?" And the pregnant lady would answer back without a beat.

Every Sunday night that winter, I would go to my dad's house, we would order Chinese food and watch *Downton Abbey* together. He'd mute the TV during commercials, but then in true Dad fashion,

MY TOP 11 GOOGLE SEARCHES
WHILE PREGNANT

1. Charlie horse leg cramp 32 weeks pregnant. And 33 weeks. And 34 weeks.

2. How much coffee can I drink if I'm pregnant? Answer: not enough.

3. Can I take a sitz bath while pregnant? And immediately after, "how to take a sitz bath."

4. Divorce attorneys in Springfield, Missouri. In the words of Liz Lemon: *blerg*.

5. Live birth video. Immediately close out of window before actual videos load.

6. Pregnant and divorced. Anyone out there? Bueller?

7. Burning vagina 37 weeks pregnant. Totally normal? Awesome.

8. What flu medicine can I take while pregnant? None. There are none. Good luck.

9. Child support formula worksheet. Double blerg.

10. Rapid heart rate, intense nausea, dizziness, 22 weeks pregnant. Just really really hungry, apparently.

11. Pregnant raw egg mayo. Like is it *really* that bad for me, cause I accidentally just bought a whole jar.

proceed to tell me the gist of each one as it aired. We would read our fortunes in terrible British accents, and one such fortune made us both leak from our eyeballs. The little sliver of white paper still sits in a dish with some jewelry on my dresser. It reads: *When the flowers bloom, so will great joy in your life.*

As much as I wanted to hide under a rock that winter, I forced myself to interact with other humans, and so I joined a women's small group at church. It was hard showing up at that first meeting knowing I'd have to explain this growing belly sooner or later, but it was so, so worth it. These ladies saw me through to the end of my pregnancy, many of them still close friends today. One girl in the group, whom I had only met once during our meetings, threw me a surprise baby shower at her apartment, and I cried A LOT of snot with those women all over the onesies. I later learned that she had gone through a divorce the year before. She helped me come out of the woods.

Sheila and my best friend, Kayla, threw me *the* most beautiful baby shower for all my friends and family a couple months before I gave birth, and I can't even look at the photos anymore because I *still* cry ugly tears when I relive those moments. I couldn't even fathom the number of people who were there — my dear friend Caroline drove eight hours from Chicago, for goodness sake. I had planned to ~~steal~~ borrow a ton of the hyacinth from my neighbor's yard for the tables, and her bushes literally only bloomed the week of the shower during that entire year. I will never forget that day.

And lastly, my mom. Ohhhh, my dear mother. She went with me to the labor and delivery classes, she was my nurse on-call (because she is my mother and an actual nurse), she timed contractions with me, she picked me up from work and took me to The Pizza House every single Friday night. I think the baby might have been half composed of pepperoni-pineapple pizza. She assembled nursery furniture, she made my baby registry with me, she got me into gel manicures and I never looked back. She convinced me I needed all new bedding at Target one afternoon — I obliged, and I slept much better that night. She sent me the same text every Sunday before church: "Coffee order?" and arrived a few minutes later with a vanilla latte in hand. She was my constant source of support; we laughed at the things that should have made us cry, because that's all we could do sometimes. It was exactly what I needed, and I shall stop typing now before the snot drips down into my keyboard. (Mom, I love you.)

> Life is unpredictable, it changes with the seasons. Even your coldest winter, happens for the best of reasons. And though it feels eternal, like all you'll ever do is freeze. I promise spring is coming, and with it, brand new leaves.
>
> ERNEST HEMINGWAY

———

All things considered, my pregnancy was easy. I had the usual first trimester nausea, got the stomach flu once and projectile vomited green jello all over my bathroom sink, frequently googled "charlie horse leg cramp only at night 34 weeks pregnant," and had back pain on the regular. I craved pretzels, fruit snacks, provolone Cheez-Its, bowls upon bowls of cereal, and would fight you for a cup of that good Sonic ice. Some days I felt like a beached whale, but most days I felt the most beautiful I ever had in my entire life. If you forget about all that other stuff going on, I *loved* being pregnant. Like I really, really loved growing a human inside my body. And I'm so thankful for that not-always-the-case blessing.

But unfortunately, I couldn't just forget about all the other stuff going on. I had assets to split up, child support and visitation plans to figure out, and the minor feat of naming a child with your soon-to-be ex-spouse.

Dustin and I fell into a rhythm of monthly visits to discuss all these things that you should never be discussing while you're pregnant. He would come over to the house — I guess it's just *my* house now? — sit awkwardly at the kitchen table and attempt a normal conversation. ~~Our~~ My dog Cooper sat next to my chair like a guard manning his post. Even he had chosen sides. *Good dog.*

We talked some about how we had even gotten to this point, but we didn't linger there for long. It was too painful, too fresh, and my hormones were not having it. And then came the gender ultrasound. He naturally wanted to be at that appointment, despite me banning him from all other doctor's appointments, just to avoid all that extreme awkwardness. But the ultrasound was our first glimpse at our baby — gosh, it's still hard to say *our* baby — so I gave him a pass for the day.

The further you get into doing the job alone, the more it becomes obvious that this job was designed for two.

It took some convincing, but my mom was the third wheel to our weird ultrasound party. I objected at first, not wanting to put her through the tension that would most certainly be wafting through the air, but she insisted.

"You're going to want someone to remember this moment with, because you're not going to be able to remember it with him. If it's just you there, who will you be able to celebrate with?"

She was right. And that little nugget of advice comes into play over and over again as a single mother. The built-in person with whom you're supposed to be sharing all these memories has chosen not to be there. So I quickly learned that I had to share my memories with other people. But also that most of the memories would still be just in my own mental scrapbook and no one else's. That's a hard, lonely pill to swallow, and I'm still learning how to do it. One of the joys of parenting is sharing the entire experience with another person. You validate the important milestones with each other. It's *that* important to the other parent, too. Ask any parents what they talk about on their romantic Friday night dates — the kids. They have a default person to relive every moment with, even the moments they didn't experience together. The default is still there. So, the further you get into doing the job alone, the more it becomes obvious that this job was designed for two.

When the default is gone, you have to find new ways to relive your parenting moments. Whether that's calling a friend and gushing about the cute thing your baby just did. Or taking a video of the toilet paper pulled all across the house and posting it to Instagram so your friends can laugh with you. Or writing it down for yourself to come across in 6 months or 6 years, because you're going to need that smile. *Those were the days,* you'll say. Single parenting is lonely by nature, but it doesn't have to be completely isolating.

So the three of us sat in the ultrasound room — God bless that technician who was probably confused by this weird family dynamic we had going on. *Let's get this over with. I know it's a boy, anyway.*

Like every good pregnant lady, I had googled pictures of ultrasound photos in bed the night before so I would know what I was looking for. And then the cold gel was squeezed out onto my belly, the screen clicked on, and suddenly I was staring at blobs and shapes and swirling and apparently that was a baby? I held back tears. *There he* — wait. I think I knew, but I wasn't sure.

"Well, Baby is bouncing off the walls in there, and it's hard to keep it still to tell, but you can see riiiiight there … see that?"

She typed four letters onto the screen in that unmistakable archaic ultrasound font: G-I-R-L.

A few minutes later, I sat peeing in the bathroom, just a door between me and my viewing party, and sobbed quietly into my hands as I tried to wrap my head around it. *It's a girl. A she. I have a daughter.* I didn't want them to hear me, so I flushed the toilet and ran the faucet for a few extra minutes. Images of me and a mini-me flashed around in my head like a movie montage. Holding a baby, holding a toddler's hand, then a kindergartener's. Holding my breath.

I knew as soon as I went back through that door, it would all begin. The nursery, the naming, the newborn, the whole mother thing. I had seen my child on a screen, knew instantly that she was mine, and maybe if I stayed in this bathroom forever, I could just freeze it all there. I knew the next few months and years would be hard. Like REAL hard. And the safety of this bathroom was that pause you take just before you jump off the diving board when you think, *is this the only way down?* But I had stayed as long as I could in the pause, and it was time to press play again.

I finally pulled it together to go back outside, and the one question on everyone's mind over the next few weeks was, *what will you name her?* But the one question on my mind was, *what will her last name be?* And that's not a question any pregnant lady should ever have to wrestle with.

I spent the next few weeks building my argument. Naturally, I made a pros and cons list. I felt a strong connection to my own last name, my own family heritage. My grandmother on my dad's side was a genealogy nerd and she had kindly passed the knack on to me. I dove into our family's history years earlier thanks to one of those Ancestry.com commercials, and as a result, had developed this strong connection to my name. And I wanted it to be *her* name. I would carry her, I would sacrifice my body for her, I would birth her into this world, and I would take care of her. She would be my whole world, and I wanted to stamp her with my name to prove it. I knew she would probably marry someday, and her name would change anyway. Heck, *I* would probably remarry some day, and my name would change, too. Either way, I wanted us to share a name, and I wasn't going to let that go without a fight.

Dustin was reluctant at first, but finally agreed. If it had been a boy, he probably would have pushed harder, but he saw how important this was to me, and he gave in. He made a lot of decisions that led to my does-not-look-like-it's-supposed-to pregnancy, so I'm thankful to him for giving me the last name, at least.

So on to first names. At one of our awkward monthly meetings, we decided the easiest way to start this whole process would be for me to make a short list of names I liked, and we could decide together from there. I was so convinced it would be a boy that my list of girl names was literally blank in the weeks before the gender ultrasound.

But afterwards, I kept coming back to a conversation I had with my mom in the waiting room of the doctor's office right before the ultrasound. Moments before we would first lay eyes on the Poppy-seed growing inside of me.

"If it's a girl, what if you named her Poppy? Since we've been calling her the Poppyseed, that would be cute, right?"

I shrugged it off, and stuck to my guns — *it was a boy, for sure.*

But then I saw her on the ultrasound. Not only was she a *she* — she was bouncing around, doing flips in my belly, and would hardly sit still enough for the technician to take her measurements. She was feisty and ornery, and right then I knew her name was Poppy. She lived up to it when she was stubborn coming out a few months later, she just wanted to do it "all my by self" as she proudly says now. That ultrasound was my first taste of my strong-willed girl.

After researching and narrowing, I learned that the name Poppy can be short for Penelope, and so I wrote it down on my list. And I fell in love with it. But I knew there was one more step, and so I prayed. I prayed hard about my next meeting with Dustin. I already felt such a strong connection to Penelope, and I was terrified that he would try to veto it. I scribbled some other names down on the list that I was okay with: *Ruby, Charlotte, June, Faye, Hazel* ... mixing *Penelope* into the bunch.

The night we were set to meet, February 25, 2014, I paced my house in prayer, rubbing my belly and begging the Lord to just give me this, please. *You've taken away the pregnancy and marriage that I thought I would have, so please just let me have this one thing.* I can't remember a time in my life when I felt so nervous about a single conversation. Except maybe one I had sitting on the floor at the Minneapolis airport about two years later, but let's not get ahead of ourselves.

Dustin came in, sat down, and I slid my scribbled list of names across to him. He looked it over silently for several minutes, as I sat shaking anxiously in my chair. It looked a lot like the scene a year before when we had bought a new car. We asked the salesman what the price was on that black Ford Escape, and he scribbled down a number on a scrap piece of paper and slid it across the desk to

> It's an odd thing. We live our entire lives with inherent unfathomable value, and it takes a watermelon under our shirt for others to notice it. For us to believe it.
>
> ERIN LOECHNER

us. We countered with a lower offer, and again, he took the paper back, crossed out the first number, and wrote a new one, then slid it back, upside down. We could hardly keep straight faces, it was so unnecessarily dramatic. We felt like we were meeting with a mob boss. And now, here we were, acting out the same ridiculous scene ourselves — though naming a human *did* feel a bit more dramatic than buying a car.

I thought my heart might beat straight out of my chest, onto the kitchen table. He set the paper down, looked up, and said, "I really like Penelope."

This moment of relief is one I will carry with me forever. It was the Lord saying, *I'm still here. I'm still in this with you.* I have no idea what made Dustin zero in on that name on that list on that evening, but he did, and it was the start of her.

I needed a win, and this one stopped me in my tracks. This decision was the one I was dreading, because I expected it to be a fight. How the heck do you name another human, even more so with a soon-to-be ex-spouse that feels like a stranger?! And I thought the pressure on my lady parts was intense.

But the decision taught me two things: first that the Lord knows the desires of our hearts. And second, we may be on opposite sides now, me and Dustin — but when it comes to Penelope, we're not. We're both here for her. He is just as much her dad as I am her mom. We're not on the same team anymore, but we *are* on the same side.

———

There were two other things that stopped me in my tracks during my pregnancy, and gave me a glimpse at what the future would look like for me and my Poppyseed.

The first was on December 31, 2013 — a New Year's Eve photo a friend showed me on Facebook of Dustin with another woman, and comments rolling in with phrases like "cute couple" and "so happy for you."

The second was on July 5, 2014 — four days before I gave birth — when my mother got up to go to the restroom with my nieces at Chipotle, and my brother and sister-in-law quickly leaned in and told me they were moving eight hours away to Nashville, Tennessee — oh, and did I want to move with them?

CHAPTER THREE

THE BiRTH

God is in the midst of her, she will not be moved;
God will help her when morning dawns.

PSALM 46:5 (ESV)

My friend Lacey sat across from me at a Panda Express a few months before my due date, and she told me that no matter how uncomfortable you feel holding someone else's newborn baby, when the doctor hands you your own, you will know exactly what to do. You won't be nervous or hesitant or unsure of where to put your hands or scared her head will just roll right off. You'll instinctively put one hand under the base of her neck, steadying her head so she can look right into her mama's eyes. And you'll know to put your other hand in that sweet spot between her round little bottom and the small of her back. You'll know exactly how to transfer her from one arm to the other without thinking twice. You'll instantly master the pass off to friends and family, and the return will come naturally, as she slides right back into your hands as if locking in that last puzzle piece. Lacey was right: I knew exactly what to do when it was my own.

> No matter how uncomfortable you feel holding someone else's newborn baby, when the doctor hands you your own, you will know exactly what to do.

Poppy's due date came and went in the summer of 2014 — she was doing this her way, and everyone else would just have to deal with it. I love hearing other mothers' birth stories, because often times the birth matches the personality of the child. Poppy came into the world with gusto. She made me wait nine days past my due date, that stubborn little thing. And just when I thought my natural birth was pretty average and uneventful, Poppy had to make sure we all knew that she was still calling the shots, here.

———

When my mom and I arrived at the hospital, there was a *People* magazine laying on the table next to the bed in my delivery room with a headline that read "Hollywood's Hottest Bachelors!" We had a good laugh about the irony of the reading material provided to the single lady giving birth, and thought we'd have plenty of time that night to discuss why Ryan Gosling was way better than Zac Efron.

I sheepishly handed the nurses my birth plan neatly typed out, with the caveat that I, of all people, was well aware that things do not always go as planned. I explained why my mother was my birthing partner, and why my actual husband would be waiting in the hallway. I was blessed with the sweetest nurse, Tasha, who read every word of that birth plan and listened carefully to my keep-the-husband-in-the-hallway instructions, showing zero judgement. She explained the situation to each new nurse that entered the room, sparing me many awkward conversations. She would proudly tell them that *Dad's in the hall, Nana's in here, and that's how it's gonna be,* giving me a supportive wink.

I was nine days overdue, and my amniotic fluid was getting low, so my doctor scheduled me to be induced on the morning of July 9th. But I was going natural with this birth, due to a spinal fusion back surgery I had when I was in high school. An anesthesiologist who looked at my x-rays a few weeks prior determined that an epidural would shoot right into my scar tissue and wouldn't do a thing. I had already wanted to do a natural birth, so this was a nice little shove off the cliff that forced me to follow through. And since an induction with Pitocin is known to cause more intense contractions, I opted to go in the night before and try a cervix softening method first.

(And this is the point in this book where my dad and brothers and anyone who closes their eyes while watching *Grey's Anatomy* are free to skip ahead a few sections. Spoiler: Poppy is, in fact, born at the end of all this.) Ok, on to the cervix.

Without diving deep into the bowels of gynecology (slight pun intended), the cervix softening method was basically a tampon-like ribbon with some medication on it that would stay all up in your lady business for 12 hours straight with the goal of softening your cervix and starting contractions naturally. The nurses didn't think it would do much for my case since I wasn't really showing any signs of labor, yet. *You'll just sleep tonight, honey,* they said. *Get some rest, and we'll start Pitocin at 6:00 in the morning,* they assured me.

Those poor nurses failed to realize that Poppy was the one in charge of this birthday show, and she would be calling the shots, thank you very much. The ribbon thingy accidentally fell out after just two hours (although I like to think that Poppy kicked it out), but it had already done the trick — I was dilated to two centimeters, and I was slowly starting contractions on my own. Poppy was finally ready, and she told my body so. Things were moving quickly, and just two more hours later, somewhere around Jimmy Fallon's monologue, I was already at 7 centimeters. Another hour later, Seth Meyers at his desk and another centimeter. The doctor broke my water around 2:00 am, and my mom made the call to the three people I wanted on the other side of that door — my dad, my sister-in-law Sheila, and my best friend Kayla — and the one person who was also supposed to be there — Dustin. I would gladly handle the childbirth, as long as I didn't have to be a part of that awkward party of four out in the hall.

Tasha had me trying every position in the book — I bounced on the birthing ball, I sat up on my knees, I did pull-ups in sync with contractions on a bar across the bed, I turned around backwards and hung over the top, searching for any way to get comfortable. I traded a promise not to push if I could have a few minutes alone in the bathroom to let my body rid itself of any remaining pizza I had eaten at my niece's bowling birthday party earlier that evening. The whole charade was long, and it was hard, and I see now why they call it labor.

At 3:00 am, just 6 hours after the whole cervix softening trick, I had reached 10 centimeters, and my body was ready to push. The nurses took bets on how fast this baby would be out, most of them putting their imaginary money on the 30 minute mark. I glanced at the clock to left. *She'll be here in 30 minutes. I'll meet my daughter in 30 minutes.*

But once again, Poppy was doing this her way. I started pushing, bearing down with a strength I didn't know I had. I squeezed my mom's hand on the left, and a nurse's hand on the right. I kept my eyes closed, and tried to focus on mind over matter. *The pain is gonna keep getting worse, Kels, so you've gotta be okay with it now.* Thirty minutes came and went, and Poppy still hadn't made her debut. We figured out that my pelvis was angled in a way that forced Poppy to move down through the birth canal, before coming back up — like she had to dip below a limbo pole. A posterior cervix, for those taking notes. With each push, I could move her to just underneath that imaginary pole, but couldn't get her far enough to pop back out on the other side. She would slide back and forth on each push, like she was just chilling on a swing set — two steps forward, one step back.

We played this back and forth game, pushing for the next three hours solid. It was the longest and quickest three hours of my life. I didn't dare look at that clock in my peripheral during those three hours, knowing it would only discourage me. I didn't dare open my eyes during those three hours, knowing it would break my concentration to count how many people in the room could see my hoo-ha. Maybe if I squeezed my eyes shut hard enough and long enough, they would all disappear, and it could just be me and Poppy. It would always just be me and Poppy.

Three hours into pushing, and still Poppy couldn't dip under that limbo pole. We were trying all of our weird positions again, but we just couldn't get her through that last dip out. It was nearly 6:00 in the morning, and the doctor on call came in with the ultimatum. He could see my exhaustion from three hours straight of pushing without medication, and I knew it, too. He held my hand and told me he believed I could do this on my own. I knew I could, too, but I needed help. We decided to try a last ditch effort — a vacuum — and if that didn't work, a c-section would be the next option. When I've talked about this conversation before, some women roll their eyes and say shame on the hospitals for scaring women into c-sections when they're trying to have a natural birth. But I didn't see it like that at all, and I don't think the doctor meant it that way either. His ultimatum was my motivation. I didn't come this far for him to just put me under and cut her out. He knew he wasn't going to have to do a c-section, he just needed me to know it, too.

> For I am about to do
> something new. See,
> I have already begun!
> Do you not see it?
> I will make a pathway
> through the wilderness.
> I will create rivers in
> the dry wasteland.
>
> ISAIAH 43:19 (NLT)

For the record, I fully believe c-sections are just as much of a birth experience as a natural birth, and women who choose or require that method are just as strong and brave. Recovering from major surgery while also caring for a newborn? I can't imagine that. For me, I knew I was bringing home this baby by myself. I wouldn't have a helper at home, and so recovering from surgery and caring for Poppy on my own physically wasn't possible. The doctor's words weren't invoking fear, they were giving me my second wind.

If I thought labor pains and pushing for 3 hours was agonizing, the inserting of a vacuum into your lady parts is downright traumatic. (Sorry Dad, you didn't skip far enough.) The vacuum is shaped like an immersion blender — it looks like a long rod with a bowl on the end of it — so the widest part is the part that goes in first. The scream I let out when that thing went in was a sound I didn't know my body could produce. My sister-in-law got it recorded in the hallway outside, while she was waiting for a much more pleasant sound: a baby's first cry. She let my brother Grant listen to it exactly one time after that day, and promptly deleted it. It was a scream that haunts all of us to this day, and thankfully it came long before this thing called The Cloud.

It was around this time that my support person, my dear mother, needed her own support person. She broke down in the arms of a nurse, and literally thought I might die right there in that hospital bed. The machine next to me started beeping, letting us all know that the next contraction was coming. I knew this was going to be the last push I had in me. My body was giving out, and I was giving it every last ounce of strength I had. I remember putting my hand to my chest, squeezing my eyes shut, and praying to God to set her there. *Set her right here on my chest, Lord, cause I'm done. This is all I have left.*

The contraction came, they flipped the vacuum switch on like a Dyson on a rug covered in Cheerios, and I held my breath. My belly hardened like a rock and every muscle in my body came together to give Poppy my last push. *I'm not coming up for air until she's out,* I made a pact with God. *I'm not breathing until she breathes. I'm not breathing until she breathes.*

I always thought birth stories were just the mother's story of giving birth. But really it's the mother and baby working together to make it all happen. It's like your first act as mother — to move your body and use every ounce of grit to push her out. And it's her first act as child — to twist and turn and wiggle her way through these small spaces to reach the outside. If you look up the phrase "give birth" in the dictionary, it offers a synonym — *give rise*. Each of you is bringing your best to the table to give rise to this new beginning. You're starting something here. There's a rising up that takes place. A rising of your heart — you didn't know it could hold so much love for one tiny human. And a rising of your power as a woman — you just pushed another human out of your body. You give rise to this new life, and you gift the world with her existence. She will leave your body, and she will take pieces of you with her everywhere she goes. She will be your heart outside your body, and she will change how you think about everything. A birth story is not just a tale of labor pains and pushing, it's a rising up of a woman to see the strength she didn't know she had.

At 6:01 am on July 9, 2014, Poppy's head, neck, shoulders, and little wet body slipped right out of me, and let out the sweetest cry. My hand still on my chest, I fell back into the bed and took my breath after hers. The doctor held up her tiny body proudly for the room to gawk, while my mom cut the umbilical cord. They laid her on my chest, right where I had been waiting for her to be all night. Her gaze was bright and alert, and she locked eyes with me for a good 10 seconds while the whole room faded away. It was just me and her. *I'm your Mama, Penelope Rose. It's me and you, now.*

————

MY TOP 6 OUTFIT ASSOCIATIONS

1. The tan H&M sweater with the not-quite-long-enough sleeves, and those old ratty black leggings. I threw it on before I drove over to my mom's house to spill my beans on that first October 21st.

2. The well-loved, hand-me-down Notre Dame sweatshirt, passed down from my brother in the 90s. I was wiping snot all over its sleeves while telling that same brother about my broken marriage.

3. The black jersey maternity dress from Target. I wore it almost every single day, even slept in it at night, the entire last month of pregnancy, because it was July in the Midwest.

4. The blue and red floral blouse that always felt a little too bright for my taste. It was my courtroom divorce outfit, and I never wore it again.

5. The famous-to-just-me-and-my-mother olive green "birthing skirt", purchased on Etsy, with the full slit up both sides for easy access to, ya know, push a baby out. I wore it proudly in the delivery room because those stiff hospital gowns were a hard *no* for me. The nurses laughed at first, but they were slow clapping by the time they caught the baby. Long live the birthing skirt.

6. The black and white tribal patterned sweater, with booties and leggings. It was my outfit of choice for my first date with Will. (*Who's Will?* Just you wait.)

The parts of a birth story that they fail to mention to new moms is the part *after* the baby comes out, when they have to stitch up your nether regions while you try not to squeeze that new baby you're holding. And also the catheter. Attention new moms: this part is possibly just as painful as the birth because your adrenaline is gone, and you can feel aaaaall the things.

A birth story is not just a tale of labor pains and pushing, it's a rising up of a woman to see the strength she didn't know she had.

There are other strange parts of the process they don't tell you about, too. Like when your husband is finally allowed in the room, and you hand him the baby that you equally share, but you feel like you've done a little more work for than him. *Bittersweet* doesn't scratch the surface. I could hardly watch him holding her; the pain of that moment overwhelmed me. You could cut the tension in that room with a knife—we all felt the heaviness of it. It was the beginning of a long journey that I am still on today — one where I am learning how to co-parent with a stranger who has hurt me deeply.

The hospital stay was more of the same — the highs of my first sweet moments as a mother, and the lows of changing bloody pads in the bathroom while your estranged husband shows off your baby to his roommates just outside the door. It was weird, and it was hard, and did I mention it was really, really weird? I shelved my anger towards him as best I could, welcomed his family into my room with the best fake smile I could muster, and tried to give him the benefit of the doubt. He was enamored with Poppy, and I did my best to let him have those moments with her.

It's the strangest reality, and every mother will agree with me on this, when the hospital just sends you home with this tiny new baby and no instruction manual. They push your wheelchair out to your car, give a thumbs up to the car seat installation you spent hours agonizing over, and then wave as you drive your precious child out onto the road. And how have you never noticed how dangerous these roads are? Cars just whizzing by only feet away from your helpless child; how is this even a thing? You swear never to leave your house again.

My mom and I drove home with Poppy, but needed to make a very important pit stop — burgers. Like really good, juicy burgers from a good place. Not road trip McDonald's burgers, we're talking real, taste-the-charcoal, wipe-mustard-off-your-pants burgers. So we took Poppy through her first drive-thru experience at the delicious Backyard Burgers. My mom was in the front seat, yelling our enunciated order into the broken speaker for the fourth time, and I was in the back seat on my phone with my nearly-deaf grandmother as she tried to settle on a time to come meet her new granddaughter.

"Let's do 3:00, Grandma."

"2:00?" she asks.

"No, 3:00!" I say louder into my phone.

"2:00?" she says again, not hearing me over my mom's burger ordering struggles.

"THREE, Grandma. One, two, THREE o'clock."

"Two? One, two?"

"One, two, THREE!"

"Two o'clock?"

I gave up. "Yep, see you at 2:00, Grandma."

It was a scene from a *Mary Tyler Moore* episode, and my mom and I laughed in that drive-thru line until we cried and woke up the baby. And this is kind of what parenthood is, yes? Trying to plan it all out, stick to the schedule, don't veer from the notes. But your baby or your toddler or heck, your teenager, has her own ideas about what the plan should be, despite your enunciated yelling into the speaker. And sometimes it's easier to just choose not to fight that battle. Throw your hands up and say, *fine you can sleep in my bed. Whatever, just eat Goldfish for dinner, I don't care. Sure, 2:00, Grandma.*

Grandma will show up promptly at 1:50 pm, she'll squeeze those cheeks, you'll take misty-eyed photos, and then everyone will go about their day. The world didn't end. We'll try again with that whole schedule thing or sleeping-in-your-own-bed thing or eating-an-actual-dinner thing tomorrow. One day at a time, Mamas. One day at a time, is how you get through this weird, foggy season. You do your best to keep the kids alive until bedtime, and then you get a quick break to catch your breath, and start again in the morning.

When Poppy was just a few weeks old, my brother Grant stopped by my house with my niece Emilee while they were out on a little date. They came in quietly as I was bounce-pacing the living room, trying to get Poppy to sleep. Emilee patted her head, gave her a kiss, and scampered off to play with my dog. Grant sat down on the couch, and asked a very simple question, "How are you doing, Sis?" A simple question that triggered some weird hormone machine inside me, and I lost it, bursting into tears. I could hardly form words with my mouth, let alone my brain. I was exhausted and embarrassed and did I mention exhausted?

I finally muttered through the snot and baby bouncing, "This is really, really hard."

Remember that one thing you must know about Grant, that I mentioned a while back? Compassion is not a strength of his. He's practical, pragmatic, and consoling a crying new mother, even if it's his little sister, is just not his cup of tea. But he muttered out something that probably felt silly to him, but it has been the best advice anyone has ever given me about parenthood.

"It gets easier," he said. And paused.

" ... and then it gets harder again." Another pause.

"And then it gets easier again ... and then harder again." We both started to laugh.

"And it kind of just keeps going like that ... forever."

Simple, but oh so true. Parenthood is this weird rollercoaster that you can't get off of. But you willingly waited in line to ride, and deep down you really don't want to get off anyway. No matter if you're on your first kid or your fifth kid, married or single or separated or divorced. Parenthood ebbs and flows, so just ride it out.

When you're in a season of The Hard, find hope in knowing that The Easy is coming up next. *Who knew that shaking up a bottle of formula was so much easier than breastfeeding! Oh, but now her poop is different and cloth diapering is losing its charm.* And when you're deep in The Easy, enjoy this blissful season and keep your survival kit handy, because the other shoe may drop soon. *Oh, thank the good Lord she is finally potty trained. Wait, why is the toilet clogged with half a roll of toilet paper? Two squares, sweetie, two squares.*

The easy is dished out right along with the hard, and so begins the journey of learning to be a parent. But don't misread this as the often unhelpful advice, *it is what it is*. There's not a phrase in the English language that I hate more. The rollercoaster is not just *how it is, so get used to it.* The rollercoaster reminds you that the track isn't one speed, one direction. It gives you hope to climb up to the top of that peak, and see the next peak out ahead of you on the track — even if there is a big dip in-between. Things won't always be how they are now. And things won't always be how they used to be, either. Don't just cross your arms and accept that roller coasters are all the same. Put your hands up, feel the wind on your armpits (yeah, I said it), and ride out the twists and turns — they're temporary.

————

Before I was thrust into caring for a newborn solo, I did have a live-in partner for a full glorious week, and that fabulous human was my mother. And I don't think I would have survived that first week without her. I woke up that first morning to a full nursing-mom-sized breakfast waiting for me in the kitchen. (I say "woke up" loosely, having been up every couple hours all night to feed the baby, like you do.) She did my grocery shopping, washed my dishes, folded my laundry, cuddled with Poppy so I could nap and shower, helped soothe her in the middle of the night, changed a million diapers, took out the trash, cooked meals, prepared snacks, and even spread out bags of frozen peas on my swollen legs and rubbed my sad sausage feet.

She was a godsend, and Mom, I am forever grateful for your help that week. (And always, duh.)

Though she lived just 10 minutes away, her leaving me and little one-week-old Poppy on that last day was a very hard goodbye. I knew I would see her the next day, but watching her walk out

> Parenthood is this weird rollercoaster that you can't get off of. But you willingly waited in line to ride, and deep down you really don't want to get off anyway.

that door with her suitcase felt like I was officially a mother. Like I had completed my one-week training, and she was pushing me off into the real world. I didn't feel ready, I didn't want her to go, but I knew it was time to do this thing on my own. There were plenty of false starts and just-one-more kisses and *okay, really I have to go now*, but eventually she made her exit. I stood in my living room like it was the edge of a cliff, frozen with swaddled Poppy looking up at me with her big brown doe eyes. *What now, Mom?* I imagined her thinking. *Just me and you now, kid.*

We managed our first few days truly alone, and I felt like I was kicking some serious motherhood butt. I stayed on top of the feedings and the diapers and the naps and the whole newborn game. I was solid for a good two days, and then I crashed. My poor mother — have I mentioned she's a saint? — could tell I was starting to wobble, and she came over one evening to let me rest. *I'm just gonna lay down for a few minutes, and then I'll be good. You won't have to stay long,* I promised her.

I remember retreating to my room and barely having the strength to even lay down on my bed — the obvious thing my body was shouting at me to do. I lay down on the very edge, as if an elephant was already in there asleep, hogging the covers. I'll never forget thinking that it was the most comfortable bed I had ever felt. *Like, I do not remember my bed being this comfortable. Has my bed always been this cloud-like? This is literally like a cloud, I can't even describe the soft ... this bed ... cloud ... elephant.* I was out like a milk-drunk baby.

I woke up about five hours later to my mom gently shaking me awake, saying it was midnight and she should probably go home since she has to work tomorrow, and I should probably feed the baby cause it's been, ya know, five hours. I'll never forget the shock I felt for having been asleep for that long. I hadn't moved a muscle — the imaginary elephant was still hogging the bed, and I was still dangling on the edge.

That was the only night I had to call in the reinforcements. I was a new woman after that five hour elephant nap, and Poppy and I finally started to get into our rhythm. We took it one day at a time, slow and steady. I tried to remember to give myself grace, which can be a tall order for this perfectionist. It was a bittersweet season with that little doe-eyed girl — sweetness in those new mom moments that seem to take your breath away, coupled with bitter reminders that this job is meant for two.

Nothing shows you that parenting is meant to be a two person job more than caring for a newborn by yourself. Everything is a reminder that you are one person. *I can do one thing at a time,* I said to crying, weeks-old Poppy while I warmed up her bottle. *I am one person,* I still tell her today when we walk in the front door and she immediately asks me for a snack and a drink and an episode of Peppa

Pig and can you hold my teddy and take off my coat, and what does she think this is, a Holiday Inn?

I envied the moms that had a partner clocking in at 5:00 pm every evening. I was jealous that they could cook dinner, while their kid was safe in the other room with another adult. My only option was a 70-pound border collie named Cooper, who was very smart, but had trouble unscrewing bottles with his paws and often confused *folding* the clean laundry with *sleeping* on the clean laundry. But for the past few years, he's been my sidekick, my bed-hogger, my security system, and my co-parent. A common characteristic for border collies is that they need a job to do — so when Dustin left, Cooper had a big one.

He took on his duties from the moment I brought home Poppy. He sniffed excitedly all over her car seat when he met her, and licked her cheek gently. He knew this was the little creature that had been growing inside of me. He immediately wanted to go outside, and as I opened the door, he ran out into the middle of the yard, threw his fluffy head back and howled the loudest I've ever heard him howl. He reserves howling for fire trucks and ambulances, but today, he had an announcement to make. His little sister had arrived, and he had a new job.

Cooper slept outside her door most of the time when she was a baby, and would go in to sit next to her crib in the mornings, keeping her company until I came in to relieve him. He gladly cleaned up the floor around her high chair at every meal, and when she was old enough, he became her playmate. She'll flop blankets across his back and pretend he's a horse. She'll hang her necklaces over his head and call him Princess Cooper. She'll pretend she's on a pirate ship with all her stuffed animals, and he is her Boat Dog. And when they're both worn out from all the shenanigans, his curled up, fluffy body becomes her pillow.

And so the two person job of taking care of a baby became a two creature job — one human and one dog. He's resting up on the couch next to me now, waiting for his little sister to get home from her dad's house, so he can get back to work.

———

I always thought I'd be the hovering new mother who creeps on her baby while she's sleeping to make sure she's still breathing. Pulling her bassinet into my room, standing over her crib, and watching for the rise and fall of her little chest through the swaddle blanket. Putting my finger softly on her lips to feel the air going in and out of her sweet little nose. But I was one person, and *I'm way too tired for that game,* I remember mumbling on that first night at home. I swaddled her up tight, plopped her down in her own crib in her own room, kissed her goodnight, and said a prayer. *Lord, I can't do this alone. I can't hover over her, I can't check on her all night, I don't even have any strength left to worry about her right now. Guard her tiny body tonight. Keep her breathing, keep her sleeping, keep her right here until I get back.*

The Lord guarded her that night, and every night. I had trusted Him this far into this weird new life of mine, and I was too tired to think about any other option. Ever since that very first bedtime, I leave her in His hands each night — *guard her when I can't be with her.* I prayed it again the first time Dustin took her out of the house on his own at six weeks. *Guard her when I can't be with her.* I prayed

it again when he kept her overnight at his house for the first
time when she was nine months
old. *Guard her when I can't be with
her.* I pray it every day she's not
under my roof.

It's a tricky thing when the
person who broke your trust
so deeply is the one person you
have to relearn to trust with your
most prized possession. You're
passing a *child* back and forth,
not some well-worn book you
think the other might like to read. It's one thing to divorce *after* kids,
when you had parented together *before*. Dustin and I didn't get that
chance. He left before the parenting even started, so it was no easy
task to hand him a newborn and watch him drive away with her. I
put my hand on the door after I closed it behind them that day, and
I prayed *hard*. It was just a couple hours, but it felt like an eternity.
I prayed he would keep her safe, I prayed he would know what to
do when she cried, I even prayed that she wouldn't be scared, being
away from her mother. I knew this was just the beginning — the first
of countless handoffs in the years to come. *Get used to it, Kels, I told
myself the first few times. This is just the beginning.*

When most moms are reading up on sleep training and nipple
confusion, I was signing divorce papers in my attorney's office, a
three-week-old baby asleep in her car seat on the floor next to me. I
rocked it back and forth with my foot, as I flipped through parenting

plans and custody agreements. I held back tears —both real and hormonal — as I tried to answer questions like, *do you want to have her on odd years or even years for Easter? And, how much is your laptop worth as an asset?* I steadied my hand to sign my name —*which last name do I use? Should I wake her up now for a feeding or see if she stays asleep until I get home? Should I change her diaper first? Would an attorney's office have a baby changing station? How did I end up here?*

Somewhere in the handoffs of our newborn baby, we negotiated child custody and visitation schedules and child support amounts. And when Poppy was just three months old, our divorce was finalized before a judge on our randomly assigned court date — October 21, 2014, a year to the day after he left. It was dumping rain that day, grey and gloomy. *Nice touch, Big Guy.* Our negotiations only lasted a few months, compared to some I had met at that mandatory divorce class who had years under their belts. What a bummer to have to teach a divorce class, right? Or maybe more bummer to be ordered by a judge to attend one? Either way, not the most uplifting way to spend a Thursday night.

I dropped off Poppy at my friend Christian's house and drove to the courthouse in the pouring rain. I was in a haze as my attorney briefed me on what would happen once we were in the courtroom. It was more of that talking head thing with no sound. My anxiety was through the roof, and I thought for sure I was going to puke. I don't remember much except sitting on the hard wooden pew while other cases came before the judge, one at a time. Dustin and his attorney were sitting nearby, and when they called up our case, I made eye contact with him for just a second. Do you smile in a moment like that? Smirk? Signal to him with one of those toy-gun points and wink? Have I mentioned, yet, how weird all of this is? I have?

I think I just gave him one of those, *well, here we are,* looks. The one where you don't really smile, you just sort of purse your lips together, and maybe shrug a little. *Here we are.*

Ironically, the nerves felt rather familiar — like the ones you feel in the moments before you walk down the aisle at your wedding. Except in place of the joy and excitement, there is bitterness and anger and grief. The undoing of something that you thought would be forever. But it all led up to this: it's ending. A wedding aisle and a courtroom aisle have an eerily similar set up.

And so we stood in front of the judge and all the anonymous witnesses behind us, and we did the dissolving. The water was murky, the salt was swirling. I sat in my car in the parking lot for awhile after the deed was done. I cried and I prayed and I watched the rain trickle down my windows and I cried some more. I waited for the rain to clear — the salt to settle back to the bottom — and I drove back to pick up Poppy.

You grieve the expectations you had for your life. You've heard stories of marriages falling apart, families splitting in two, but you reassure yourself that it'll never be *your* story. But then your marriage slips through your fingers faster than you can catch it, and you're thrust into single motherhood against your will at the ripe old age of 26. Your story has taken a turn, and you can't go back to rewrite it. The grieving of that bulldozed expectation is a battle you'll fight for a long, long time. But the conscious, joyful welcoming of this new life you're on the brink of, is a battle you must fight *for*. The sting of comparison will tell you that your life is *less* than because of that thing that changed your story. That toxic relationship or that child with a disability or that struggle with infertility or that surprise diagnosis or that job you lost or that death you can't shake.

The hand you were given is far different than what you expected — but the good news is, the game isn't over. In fact, new cards were just dealt, and it's just begun. You can discard those expectations that no longer fit in your story, and you can draw new cards. New perspectives, glass half-full attitudes, the practice of gratitude. Joyfully welcoming the chance to start this new game, despite the uncertainty of where it might lead. Begin again. There is no shame in starting over.

CHAPTER FOUR

THE MOVE

"You can be shattered, and then you can put yourself back together piece by piece. But what can happen is this: You wake up one day and realize that you have put yourself back together completely differently. ... And no matter how hard you try, you simply cannot fit into your old life anymore."

GLENNON DOYLE

So there we are, sitting outside at Chipotle, in the hot July sun. I was six days overdue, and if one more person asked me what my due date was, I might have punched them. I was stuffing myself with the extra guacamole when my mom got up to take my nieces to the bathroom. My brother Grant waited until she was a safe distance away, and leaned in across the table.

"Kelsey, we need to tell you something. Sheila take it away." He turned to put his wife on the spot, as he loves to do with big news, and she blurts it out.

"We're moving to Nashville!"

I froze mid-bite and gave the slight head turn to the right that says, *ummm ... excuse me?*

I was a little confused — we were all born and raised right here in Springfield, and they had shown no signs of wanting to leave. It felt a little out of left field, but I also wasn't *that* surprised. Grant and Sheila are adventurous. They loved going on exotic vacations, showing their three daughters the value of travel and experiencing new places, and so why wouldn't they pick up and move to a new city for no particular reason? It kind of sounded like something they'd do, so as sad as it made me to think of them being more than 15 minutes away, I had to be on board.

But the second thing they said took me a bit longer to come around to:

"We want you and Mom to come with us."

That got a double slight head turn to the right that said, *okay, now ya'll are legit crazy.*

But they were serious. And when they told Mom just a few minutes later after her bathroom break, she was in shock. Good thing we sat outside. Her initial reaction to all of it was a big fat *NO. No, you can't take these three granddaughters away from me. No, you can't leave me and your sister here.*

And then it turned to, *no, I can't leave my job after 37 years. No, no one's going to hire a 60-year-old nurse set to retire in a few years. No, I can't leave my aging parents. No, I can't sell my house.*

I was set to deliver a baby any day, and so a move to another city for no apparent reason than to follow my family there should have been the last thing on my mind. But it quickly moved its way to the front of the line. Being single again was settling in as my new normal, and I was thinking about what dating would look like down the road. My business was growing and changing, and like

Grant's desire to plant himself in Nashville, it was a city ripe with an entrepreneurial community. A city for dreamers with a plethora of connections and opportunities. Every corner of Springfield reminded me of Dustin, and so a new city maybe wasn't *that* crazy of an idea.

There were a lot of questions. But that evening, my mom and I found ourselves in Poppy's soon-to-be nursery researching housing costs in Nashville. We opened up Google Maps and Zillow, we pulled out calculators, and we said over and over to each other, *are we really going to do this?*

> I will guide you along the best pathway for your life. I will advise you and watch over you.
>
> PSALM 32:8 (NLT)

And so we made this mother-daughter pact — *if you go, I'll go,* we promised each other. It felt wild, it felt a little reckless, it felt like the exact thing I needed to jump start this new life in which I had found myself. *Why yes, I'll move out of the town I've lived in for the last 26 years and off to a city I've never even been to.* Totally normal.

———

Somehow — and it can really only be what they call "a God thing" — we managed to sell two houses in Springfield, rent the perfect house in Nashville, pack up the two old houses and move them into the one new house a state away, all in just six months. It was a logistical nightmare, but we hunkered down with our monstrous to-do lists, our rolls upon rolls of packing tape, and the puzzled look of those we loved. *You're moving where? And why?*

I have a weird connection to the houses I live in. I can almost remember every address, and what season of life each home housed me for. The little stone cottage on Stewart was the home Dustin and I bought together, and the one I sold alone. A couple nights before I moved out, I sat down on the stairs and read every entry from the original abstract that the previous owners passed on to me. If you're not an old house lover like me, an abstract is the booklet that records every time the property trades hands — every buy, sell, gift, and inheritance. This abstract was just for the land the house was sitting on, and spanned from the mid-1800's up until 1950, the year the house was built.

I sat carefully flipping through the fragile, yellowed pages, and noticed a pattern right away. The majority of the land owners had this label next to their name: "unmarried woman." I sat back, stunned. This house was passed down from single woman to single woman, in an era when owning property was obviously rare for any kind of woman, much less the unmarried kind. I suddenly felt even more connected to these old walls. And honored that the woman I had sold it to, the one moving in that weekend, was a single mother of two. And so I sat down and wrote her this letter:

Hi Kelly!

I just wanted to write you a quick welcome note and let you know what a special house you have here. I bought this house as a happy young married woman, and I'm leaving it a newly divorced single mom with a completely different story than I expected. My entire life changed under this roof, and it will always hold a special place in my heart. I hope when you sell it some day, you can say the same. I think it's pretty cool that it's being passed on to another single mom.

I hope you enjoy this beautiful home with your kids; it's been such a great little cottage for me and my little one (and my dog!). The backyard is like heaven in the summer — there are blackberries, strawberries, and raspberries in the small area on the north fence. The stone structure in the back makes a great grill. The garden is perfect for vegetables — the neighbor Jim and his dog Ralph can give you some pointers! The hydrangeas under the sunroom windows and the knockout roses in the front yard will be blooming soon. This is a wonderful home to start this new chapter of your life.

Happy moving, and welcome home!

Kelsey, Penelope, and Cooper the dog

I left the note on the kitchen counter next to a jar full of hyacinth from the neighbor's bushes along the fence, the same ones I borrowed for my baby shower the year before. I closed the door on that house and that chapter, fairly certain the new owner probably thought I was some sentimental weirdo.

I don't know how to quite describe it, but leaving that house I loved, and the city I had lived in my entire life, just felt right. I was standing at the end of a long road behind me of a broken marriage, a painful divorce, and now this baby in one arm and no partner on the other. I had no idea what was coming next, but when Nashville came rolling out onto the table that afternoon at Chipotle, it didn't take long for me to say yes. It felt like I had looked down at the end of that road, standing on the edge of the pavement, and someone had

> My spiral staircase of progress means that my pain will be both behind me and in front of me, every day. I'll never be "over it," but I vow to be stronger each time I face it. Maybe the pain won't change, but I will.
>
> GLENNON DOYLE

kindly placed a stepping stone a few inches in front of me. It was the natural next place to land — a very hard to explain step that I was willing to take.

And even now, as I sit in a beautiful home that I never want to leave — in Springfield, Missouri — I know that Nashville was the place I was supposed to be. I know that four days before Poppy was born was the exact day Grant and Sheila were supposed to tell us their big plans, and that we were supposed to say yes when they invited us along. I know that Nashville was the start of a new life, but not its resting place — instead, it was the holding place.

———

In the book *I Am Amelia Earhart,* the author contrasts the real events of the last weeks of the famous pilot's life with a fictional narrative of what might have been, had her plane crash landed on an island and Amelia survived. And that middle space among what we know as fact and the story we like to imagine — she calls this time the *between.* "The between voyager travels through uncharted territory, navigating dangers, attempting passage into the next life." And she reminds us that it's in this space that "we are open to the slightest shifts, when our powers are acute, when we can change the future."

On July 9, 2015 we celebrated Poppy's first birthday among packed up boxes in a furniture-less house, and just a week later drove our U-haul out of Springfield. I remember driving across southern Missouri and crossing over into the rolling hills of western Tennessee. With my baby and my dog in the backseat, I was literally in my *in-between*. The cold hard facts of my old life behind me, and a still-just-imaginary life out ahead of me.

A few years later, I would sit on my best friend Kayla's couch in front of a roaring winter fire, and she would tell me about a prayer someone had prayed over her, and they had used an unfamiliar term: "changing tack."

It was a sailing term describing the moment when you sense the winds are about to change, and you adjust your sails just before, so that they catch the wind right when it shifts, and your vessel changes direction. Kayla and I are avid planners, and so we sat there that evening talking about what it's like to do the opposite. To take risks rather than make plans. To let go of the reins. To change tack, and let the wind carry us on to the next thing, even if we couldn't quite see what it was.

As planners, we eventually found ourselves talking about calendars and dates, and Kayla shares this weird thing with dates that I have (one of the many reasons we've been best friends since fifth grade). I asked her how she visualizes her year, and how she sees the coming months of the year in her head. And this is where things got interesting. For me, my year is laid out in an upside down U shape. It starts with September on the bottom left, moving straight up into December. Then January turns to the right, moves on into spring, and then July starts wrapping around clockwise ending with August on the lower right.

In Kayla's mind, her year is more like a backwards L shape. It starts with August on the bottom left, and the rest of the months wrap around counterclockwise to the top, ending with July. She told me that evening that she can always see about a year ahead of her, seeing events and trips plotted out before her, and the gaps in between. I can visualize the same on my own mental calendar. But lately, she can't see past August. September and beyond is a blur, she said, like someone wrote it on a chalkboard and then wiped their hand across it, smudging the months and milestones and the memories that were to come.

And it was around the time that she realized she couldn't see past August that this friend prayed a prayer over her about changing tack, and she was forced to be content in this in-between place, between the known and the unknown. It felt unclear, unsettled. She was changing tack, because the winds were about to shift. Three months later she was pregnant with her first child.

Since I'm so well-versed in sailing as a land-locked Midwesterner, I latched on to this term, changing tack. Adjusting your sails to take advantage of the changing winds. This felt like moving to Nashville to me. The winds were blowing that direction; it appeared that half my immediate family was moving there, so I chose to adjust my sails in accordance. I was taking advantage of where the wind was blowing, and felt sort of like I was just along for the ride. I was changing tack to catch the wind.

Driving across middle America, my old life was literally in the rearview mirror, and my new one just peeking up over the horizon.

It sounds dramatic, and that's because it was. For this introvert homebody, moving to a new state was a big deal. But that's where my wind was blowing that season. You can't control where it blows, so you might as well change tack and ride it out. Your hair might get messy, some things might fall overboard, your calendar might get smudged when the water splashes up on it. But the wind is where the adventure is. The wind is the middle, and the middle is the living.

––––––––

The first weeks and months in Nashville were bliss. I had nearly unlimited childcare as my mom was job hunting, we were exploring our new city as a family, and the whole thing felt like some big grand adventure we were all on together. It was the honeymoon phase, you could say, and there was no place I would rather have been.

A few weeks into my new city, I found myself sitting around the fire at this swanky backyard cocktail party with my one Nashville friend so far, Jill. It was a smorgasbord of maybe 20 or so women sitting around that fire, and the host, Mary, asked us to go around the circle and answer one simple question: *what was our biggest struggle in life at that moment?*

Cue the sweaty introvert palms. I felt so out of place for someone who's used to spending 90% of her evenings home alone in her pajamas watching *Grey's Anatomy*. But I could tell that God had led me to this place. It was not a coincidence that I had been invited to a last minute dinner a few weeks earlier with a handful of fellow women in online business. It was not a coincidence that a woman at that dinner invited me to this party tonight. And it was not a coincidence that when I say *fellow*, I really mean they were on page 463 and I was still fumbling around near page 30-something.

I sat around that fire expecting these women I look up to — owners of million dollar businesses, well-known musicians and authors and speakers — to have answers like, *I'm struggling with how to spend all this money* or *I can't decide which nanny to hire* or *should we build on to the east side or the west side of our house?* But to my surprise, no matter our industry or celebrity, we all mostly shared the exact same struggles.

The women who seemed like they had it all together were doubting their abilities as a mother. The women who were on the brink of making it big felt lost in their purpose or direction. The women who were so good at putting on a brave face in public were struggling with depression and crippling anxiety on the inside. Every one of us wept around the fire that night, as we realized we were really all on the same page. Our internal battles became our external connections, as we all began to really *see* one another.

It's easy for women to compare, to play the numbers game. *She's done this, I've done that, she's gotten that, and I'm stuck with this.* It's easy as a single woman without a spouse; it's easy as a married woman without a child; it's easy as a mother without a break. We look around at everyone else's paper, and we think our answers should match. But we're taking a different test than they are. Those folders and paper blinders that our grade school teachers used to make us put up during a test — those don't matter. We can look at everyone else's answers all we want, but we're not even taking the same test.

We may think we know what's best for our lives; we may think we know how it should all play out. But we're the last people that should have those answers. God sees the entire picture, we can only see this one snippet that we're living in. And He doesn't hold it all in a *look-at-all-this-control-I-have-over-you sort of way,* He holds it all in a *trust me* sort of way. *I am doing a good work,* He promises.

We look around at everyone else's paper, and we think our answers should match. But we're taking a different test than they are.

The women to our left and to our right, they have their own challenges. They answered the questions to their own test, and it's not easier or harder than the test that's in front of you. It may look really different, but it's probably more similar than you realize. Whether you're a critically-acclaimed singer-songwriter at a backyard cocktail party in Nashville, or you're the single mom trying to figure out online dating while sitting across the fire from her — your struggles are real, and they are arduous, and they are far from frivolous.

————

Sometime in August 2015, just a month after moving to Nashville, my mom came upstairs to my desk, where I was burning the midnight oil on my growing to do list, Poppy asleep in the room next to me, and she showed me a photo. It was posted on Facebook about a month earlier — the weekend we moved to Nashville, actually — and it was of Dustin and his girlfriend, Melany, proudly showing off an engagement ring following the obvious popping of a certain sacred question.

I sat unmoved in my chair, staring at this stranger in the photo, the one I used to be married to. He was beaming. *Was he so happy to be committed to someone else already?* Our divorce had been finalized for less than a year. His smile was salt in my still open wound. I didn't know how to respond, except — once again — to write. So I opened up a new note in Evernote, and I started vomiting. Words, that is. I threw up words all over my screen, stream of consciousness, until I had rid my brain of as much sting and grief and frustration as one night could handle.

I dumped out questions like, *what does she see in him? Does she know what she's getting herself into? What do her parents think of him? How much did he tell them? How much did he tell her? Did he give her a nicer ring than he gave me?* Ya know, real adult stuff.

And also — *why was this photo taken three weeks ago, and he hasn't said a word to me about it?* I mean, I understood that the ex-wife is not the first person you run to with exciting news like an engagement, but a heads up would have been nice, right? I was frustrated that his leaving was still so fresh in my mind, and I questioned how his greener pastures could come so easily.

My heart was racing from one question to the next as I tried to wrap my mind around my ex-husband getting remarried — an act I was *so* sure I would be doing first. But there he was, smiling with a new girl and a new ring, and here I was, still single and definitely Facebook stalking. I

> Take one last glance at the way things used to be. Cherish it. But let go. Life is turning. The seasons are changing. You are becoming new, again and again.
>
> ALLISON FALLON

was supposed to be the one who got snatched up again. *I was supposed to be the one who moved on and found better, not him. I was supposed to be the one who picked up my pieces first — who was okay first.*

The more I thought about their engagement, the more I thought about *her* in particular, not even him. See, I had met her just once at that point. They had come to Nashville the weekend I moved there, to visit with Poppy and some of Melany's family that lived in the area. I had seen her from afar several times in Missouri, sitting in the passenger seat of Dustin's car when he would pick up Poppy. I had seen her in that New Year's Eve photo just a couple months after he moved out. And then I met her, face to face, for the first time in a Whole Foods parking lot outside Nashville. They had gotten engaged just two days before that, but I was not privy to that information just yet, and was introduced to her only as The Girlfriend.

She was several years older than him and seemed very level-headed and mature — all of which surprised me. The first thing I noticed about her was her kind, gentle spirit. Her love for Poppy was obvious in how she held her and comforted her through the simple transition of being passed from Daddy to Mommy. She began to cry as she told me how much she cared for my child, and how she had no intention of being my replacement. She knew that I was Poppy's mother, and that she was secondary to that. I hoped they couldn't see my own tears through my sunglasses as I held Poppy in that hot July sun. And as much as I had wanted to hate the ~~girlfriend~~ fiancé, I actually really, really liked her. And I didn't quite know what to do with that.

In some ways, she reminded me of myself when Dustin and I were dating as teenagers who thought they knew everything. I wondered if she was blind to his red flags like I was — caught up in his charm and gentle, well-intentioned demeanor. I found myself worried about her — worried that she was making the same mistake I did. Worried that he would hurt her like he hurt me.

In some ways — weird, unexpected, indescribable ways — I felt almost protective of her. Sometimes, I still do. I feared for her — not that Dustin was a monster like some ex-husbands are known to be, because he has been the furthest thing from that. But I feared that he would leave stones unturned with her. He would fail to mention mistakes he had made and debts he owed; things that led to our own demise and that could help them avoid theirs. I prayed he wouldn't keep things from her like he kept them from me. I prayed that she would be spared from the same kind of pain he inflicted on me.

And so she killed me with kindness that day in the Whole Foods parking lot. She won me over pretty quickly, as difficult as it is for my stubborn self to print that in a book. And over the years of Poppy telling everyone that she has a Mommy and a Daddy *and* a Melany, I've come around to the simple fact that Melany is a big part of Poppy's life, and there is nothing I can do about that. Not as big as a Mommy or a Daddy, but she's up there. And if she's an advocate for my child, treats her with respect, teaches her kindness, and gives her another living example of love, than I have to learn to accept her as a part of this weird, pieced-together family we're all stuck in.

God has shown me a glimpse of His grace for me, in the grace that Melany has shown to me. I am forever grateful that she is the New Wife I have to deal with, if I am forced to deal with one in the first place. I am thankful for the example she is to Poppy, and I'm glad that my little bird will grow up with two strong women to look up to. It's not the family I imagined for myself — at times it feels so broken and unkempt — but it is the only one that Poppy will ever know. She may grow up and feel the comparison that so easily creeps into my heart, too — pointing at another home and thinking *that* is the type of family I should have had.

But I pray she sees the redemption story that's being written right in front of her. I pray she knows how lucky she is to have extra people that love her and are committed to taking care of her. I pray she honors, but never has to experience, the pain her parents went through to bring her into this world. And I pray that I see all of these positives, too, when the negatives seem to shout from the rooftops.

A few weeks later, Dustin finally spilled the beans that he didn't realize I had already knocked over. I acted surprised, and secretly relished as he nervously searched for the best way to tell his ex-wife that he was engaged. *An ex-wife has to enjoy some things, okay?*

> She may grow up and feel the comparison that so easily creeps into my heart, too — pointing at another home and thinking *that* is the type of family I should have had. But I pray she sees the redemption story that's being written right in front of her.

And just like that, three months later they were married. Old husband and new wife. The winds were changing, and so I started to change tack to catch it. New directions, new perspectives were waiting to be uncovered. It was a season of growing up for all of us, and in hindsight, it was just the first of many seasons that would prove a pattern of resiliency.

My friend and writer Allison Fallon writes about change and resiliency so eloquently, that her posts often get an audible *YES!* from me as I read them. After her divorce, she perfectly phrased that moment where you realize everything is about to change: "Take one last glance at the way things used to be. Cherish it. But let go. Life is turning. The seasons are changing. You are becoming new, again and again."

As a self-proclaimed sentimental junkie, the easy part is the looking back. Marking out the milestones that got you to where you're standing today. The relationship that ended, or the one that started. The job that ran its course, or the one that's just beginning. The move away from something old and into something new. Glancing back is easy; it's the letting go part that's tricky. It's the turning back towards the front and then moving on that trips me up. Accepting that things don't look quite how you expected.

And so it's a shame that all the things that drew me to Nashville in the first place — the newness of starting over — would end up being all the same things that made it nearly unbearable in the end.

CHAPTER FIVE

THE BOYFRIEND

Of all the things trauma takes away from us,
the worst is our willingness, or even our ability, to be vulnerable.

BRENÉ BROWN

The thing about dating after divorce that no one tells you about, is that you have this crippling fear that it's all going to happen again. The guy is going to up and leave at any minute, without warning or reasonable explanation. Maybe this happens with regular dating. I wouldn't know, because I married the first guy I dated. But post-divorce dating is no joke, friends. It's riddled with anxiety, and you almost never feel secure in what you have. Now maybe when you're in a relationship that's actually thriving and healthy and both parties are actually on the same page, it's different, but I've never been in one of those.

Did I just spoil the ending of this chapter for you? Sorry about that. But consider the middle. The in-between. That's where the magic happens, remember? The middle happens to be where most of us find ourselves, wandering around looking for the exit.

It was the evening of October 21, 2015. The anniversary of so many things now. It was an uneventful day that year, and I thought maybe the curse had been broken. I opened up my laptop on my bed, and settled in for my usual work hours — 8 o'clock to midnight. But I wouldn't end up getting much work done, because of that little ding of my Facebook messages.

You have a new message from Will Harper.

A simple notification that would tie me up for the next few hours — actually, the next few months. Well, the next couple *years,* really, but we're getting ahead of ourselves.

Will Harper was no one new; he was an old friend of nearly a decade. His sister was my college roommate, bridesmaid in my wedding, and I in hers. She and I were close, and her family was an extension of my own. I vacationed with all of them once — Will was there. I rang in many New Year's at her house — Will was usually there, too. I road-tripped to see her eight hours away after she transferred schools — Will and another friend came along. Will was always around. He was always kind, considerate, hilarious, and just the right amount of goofy. He was literally tall, dark, and handsome. And I was always … well … with Dustin.

And then I was engaged, and then married, and I never gave Will a second thought.

But then I *wasn't* married, and Will noticed. He sent me a message on Facebook one day, a few weeks after I had moved to Nashville — a typical *long time, no see* type message. And then he sent another. And another. And he was piquing my interest. *What was he up to?*

So the message on October 21, 2015 wasn't a huge surprise, but the conversation was shifting. Changing tack, you could say.

"What's your personality type?" he asked that night.

I hadn't taken the test, so he sent me a link to a free Meyers-Briggs test online. I immediately went through all 80 questions like the people-pleaser I am, and replied back, "INFJ. What are you?"

He wrote back, "I'm an ENFP. INFJ and ENFP are supposed to be extremely compatible."

Ooooooookay, buddy. I'm getting the hints, loud and clear now, thank you very much. I was done with the games, and I wanted a straight answer. I took a deep breath, typed out the question I had wanted to ask for weeks, hesitated over the Send button, and finally pushed it through.

"All this messaging lately, is that just old friends catching up or is it something more?"

Immediately, the three dots appeared. My heart was pounding as I watched him type. It took him only a few seconds to respond.

"Kelsey, I've had a crush on you since the day I met you nine years ago."

Whoa. His words hung in the back of my throat for a few seconds, and I re-read his line over and over. And then I burst into tears. Like, hand-over-mouth-don't-wake-the-baby tears.

Ohhhh, I see it now. It's Will. It was Will all along.

I was immediately taken back to the moment Dustin left. Sitting at the kitchen table, tears streaming down my face, watching our entire relationship rewind. I saw myself back at a literal Square One, that day. Like I was standing on a big square floor tile with a giant number one on it. But even in that deep, deep heartbreak, the Lord was so clearly telling me He had something better. He had someone better suited for me, and someone better suited for Dustin. He was saving a relationship for me that would be more than I could have ever dreamed for myself. He just had to end this one first. He amputated a limb to save the body.

Two years later, the amputation still ached because the wound was still there. But the body had been better for it. It was — and still is — slowly healing and health is being restored, and I had this sudden gut feeling that Will was part of that restoration. This is where my happy ending would start. I saw the Lord unfolding bits and pieces of my story over the last two years, and I was so sure this piece — this October 21st — was the brink of my last chapter of healing.

I was right about part of it — a shift was certainly coming. The winds were changing, just not in the direction I was expecting.

———

Will and I talked all day, every day, from then on. We texted, called, and FaceTimed as much as we could. He still lived in Springfield and I had just moved to Nashville, but we were determined to make this work. He drove eight hours to Nashville for a quick weekend visit just a week or so after that October 21st conversation.

He made reservations at my favorite restaurant, and I was floored at his ability to plan ahead and take the lead. I had never experienced this before in a partner — even a gesture as small as calling ahead.

I'll never forget that first date, because I had never felt so at home with a guy. First dates should be awkward and a little painful, but this one was the opposite. I wasn't nervous or anxious, I felt confident in myself and proud to be sitting next to him. He gave me his undivided attention, and made me feel like the most important person in the room. I will compare all future first dates to his, and for that I say sorry to any man that finds himself sitting across the table from me. Will Harper ruined this for you, so just hope for a second date.

That one weekend in Nashville would be his only weekend in Nashville, but in the moment I felt like it could be the first of a million weekends with him. We went to the movies, he opened doors, we held hands, he drove us around and paid for everything. For the first time in a very, very long time, I felt truly taken care of. I relaxed and gladly took the back seat to his leadership. I was tired of leading, and was happy to have him take over. I wish I had savored it even more than I did, because it was a season that was much shorter than I hoped it would be.

———

Remember when I said the thing about dating after divorce, is that you have this crippling fear that it's all going to happen again? This is the part of my story where that fear crept in. Not even crept in, it kicked in the front door, marched inside, and threw down a sleeping bag.

Dustin's decision to end our marriage was affecting my relationship with Will, and that pissed me off. It's like the phantom limb phenomenon of the amputation that was our marriage. I've now experienced having someone I trust completely walk away from me and betray my trust on so many levels. And now, entering a new relationship, this scared me to death. I felt like I was grasping at straws to feel assured. I hated it that another person's decision could affect things that had nothing to do with him, even years later. It felt like he had some kind of power over me, but the kicker is that Dustin didn't even have a clue. He thought it was sad and hard and I was mad, but that I had moved on. He had no clue that what he set in motion on that first October 21st had put a fear in me about any future relationship I would have with a man. Dustin had no clue how terrified I was that Will was going to do the same thing that he did.

Lord, take that burden from me. Lift it off and let me breathe soon. I know I need to learn things from it; I know it happened for a reason. I know you're still working. But please let me come up for air.

I sent up prayers like this nearly every day Will and I were together. I felt like I could never have total assurance until I was standing at an alter reciting vows and exchanging rings. I didn't want to live in fear until that moment, but I didn't know how to cope. I wanted to enjoy this season of courting or dating or whatever it was we were doing, but this fear was like our annoying third wheel. It would stomp back in the door as soon as I started to enjoy the newness of it all, or tried to savor the sappy silly things. I was afraid I was going to miss out on the experience of falling in love again, because I was too concerned it would all be gone in an instant.

I can tell the Lord was trying to teach me something during this season — about being in control, trusting in Him, and learning to let Him lead. When Dustin left, I felt completely out of control. But I had such a strong sense that that was the right decision, it wasn't so hard to let go of the reins and trust completely in God's process.

With Will, the answers weren't as clear. I didn't know for sure if he was who God had for me; I didn't know if trusting him with my whole heart was the right decision yet. And that uncertainty made it so much harder to let go of control.

It's natural to want to know how something will turn out. It's normal to be fearful of setting your hopes too high, only to have them come crashing back down.

I didn't want to be so close to something so great, and have it slip just out of reach.

I would look at Will on that screen and beg God not to let him slip away. I pined for that assurance with Will, but I knew deep down that what I really was looking for was assurance with God. To know that HE will not leave me out of the blue. To know that HE will not let my heart break again. To know that HE is in control, and not me, and that is a *good* thing.

> I was afraid I was going to miss out on the experience of falling in love again, because I was too concerned it would all be gone in an instant.

It was around this time that I started seeing a counselor for the first time in my life, and it kind of changed everything for me. I was in a new city, a new relationship, and cozying up with a new fear that had laid dormant in my heart for years. Liz, my counselor, was my constant. She was neutral, unbiased, and had zero skin in the game. I was paying her to be my friend, basically, and I was happy to write that check. I came away from our weekly chats believing that every human on earth should be in counseling at all times. Just in case. And boy am I glad I had locked her in for the next few months.

When my fears weren't front and center, Will was my warm, cozy fire that winter. He challenged me to be all kinds of better. My faith has never been stronger with the influence he had on my life. He became my instant encourager and prayer partner, and I truly believe that for that season, I needed him in my life. We read Psalms and Proverbs together daily, we had alarms set to text each other at 10:00 am to remind the other about the reading. We FaceTimed every night and talked about the parts of our day where we saw God, and the parts that were more foggy. Even now, I use that season as a benchmark — *can I get my faith back to that daily craving that he helped foster within me? Can I be that close to God again?*

While our relationship with each other seemed to blossom and bloom into something I was truly thankful for, my relationship with my family paid the price. I loved Will, and his best qualities were his intellect, his faith and leadership, and his kind spirit. But on paper, I was well aware that he didn't look great. Will had spent the last two years doing humanitarian work abroad and was just returning home, unsure of what he would do next. While that part does look good on paper, it also meant that he, of course, had no job, no car, and was living with his parents at the age of 30. Not to mention dropping out of college and recovering from a drug addiction years earlier. *I get it, okay, you don't have to point out the red flags.* But Will's life had so many more intricacies that brought him to this place. I won't get into details here of how amazing his redemption story truly is — that's *his* story to tell, and he's a gifted writer, so I'd be willing to bet it's a book someday. But he had found himself at this crossroad in his life where the next steps were unclear, and maybe I found a little comfort in that.

But still, at the end of the day, Will's answers to *where do you work?* and *where do you live?* and *what are you planning to do now?* were not the answers that parents and protective older brothers like to hear. And it was especially frustrating — and ultimately sad — for me to watch my family not truly see or understand the person I was falling in love with. I felt torn much of the time, defending him to my family and my family to him.

————

In December of that year, my family and I headed up to New York City to visit my brother, Taylor. I tried to put on a smile, but the trip was hard for me. I was feeling more and more disconnected from my family, and traveling together just felt awkward and uncomfortable most of the time. Also, I had an 18-month-old who was more than I could handle at times, and that has since been her one and only trip on an airplane. On the flight home, me and my squirmy lap child were sitting between my niece, Emilee, and my mom. I had planned Poppy's whole nap schedule around that flight time, so when we got to the airport, it was delayed. Of course.

We killed time trying to keep her awake until the new flight time, but we pushed her over the edge, and the peak of her meltdown was conveniently right as we boarded the plane. She started kicking and screaming at the top of her lungs, as I tried my best to keep her under control. Nothing would soothe her — not the pacifier, the blanket, her beloved stuffed rabbit Foofoo, her cup, or even a snack. Her arms and legs were flailing, and she was grabbing at anything she could get her hands on, clawing at my glasses and my face. Fellow moms of 18-month-olds, you know what I'm talking about. I was completely embarrassed and felt totally out of control. I was barely managing a grip on her when my sister-in-law, Sheila, came to the rescue with an iPad slipped through the seats playing *Frozen*. Poppy settled a bit when she saw it, and finally started to quiet down. Within a few minutes, she had laid her head on my chest, I slipped in the pacifier, and she fell asleep.

And that's when it was my turn to cry. Sweet Emilee quietly held the iPad in place for Poppy, and looked up at me watching floods of tears rolling down my face. And with my chin tucked down next to Poppy as if hiding from every passenger on that plane, I whispered to God, *I need a helper.*

I was thinking back to a sermon Will and I had listened to by renowned pastor, Tim Keller, about marriage. He was describing a spouse as a helper — its original meaning translated literally to *help mate*. Single motherhood was a weight I could barely shoulder during that season. I wanted a help mate so desperately, and I begged God for it daily. I was so sure that Will was going to be that helper, and felt so confident the Lord was confirming that in His own subtle, quiet ways.

———

Christmas that year was bliss. I had eleven uninterrupted days with Will back in Springfield, and it was so, so special to me. We went on nice dates, we went on simple dates, we went on walks and talks and coffee trips and Walmart errands. We met his friends, we met my friends, we did family stuff, we did normal things. We cooked together, we worshipped together, we prayed together, we told terrible jokes together. He held Poppy so I could eat a meal while it was still hot on my plate. He carried her out to the car and adorably attempted to buckle her into her carseat. We shared food, we shared cars, we shared Chapstick and mints, we shared stories, we shared fears. He opened doors, he held my coat, he drove me around, he picked up the tab. He spent way too much money and I told him so, and he replied, "I paid for things, and that's as it should be." It was realistic at times; it was completely unrealistic at times.

> Meaningful things are still happening here. Even after all these years, and everything that fell out of place, you have not fallen from grace. And you are going to be okay. Things will take time to come together, but you can still choose joy while you wait.
>
> MORGAN HARPER NICHOLS

I called him on the long drive back to Nashville with the question, "How am I different than all the others?" I wondered sometimes if I would just be another name on his list of girlfriends. I stumped him, apparently, when he said he had never thought about that and needed a few days to think it through.

A couple days later he had an answer, and looking back, that must have been when the winds were shifting. Throughout our relationship, and even in past relationships, he always prayed, *God let this work out.* But he felt that wasn't the right mindset — it was selfish and an attempt to put his own plans above God's plans. Instead, he felt that we both should be praying, *God, let Your will be done and not ours.* That was the missing link with him and his past relationships, and he said that's been the missing link with us, too. Shifting our mindset to still be open to the possibility of it not working out because maybe *that* was God's will, and learning to trust him with that possibility, will be the difference.

He thought his answer would scare me off, but I was so sure I knew God's will that I didn't flinch. In fact, it made me more sure that I knew exactly how this was all going to play out.

————

The beginning of the end was in Portland. I was there with some girlfriends and fellow business owners on our annual trip to hash out business plans for the coming year. Will had been a little distant the last couple days, but our schedules were off, and we just kept missing each other. A few days before, he had told me what I had been waiting so long to hear — he decided he was moving to Nashville. I was ecstatic, but I tried to play it cool.

But then the next day, he took a step back. He said he wanted to be 100% sure this move would be the right choice, so he was going to take a week to pray about it. My heart sank a bit, and I was afraid he'd change his mind, but I was still hopeful.

So on my second to last day in Portland, we finally got our schedules to line up and I gave him a call. I could tell something was on his mind right away, and my heart beat a little faster. He had been talking with friends and family and mentors about Nashville, and they all agreed with the good reasons to move there … but …

My heart sank at that "but." I was sitting on the front porch of our Airbnb in a rocking chair, watching the infamous Pacific Northwest rain. I closed my eyes and held my breath at the "but."

Please God, don't do this.

He told me he had been feeling less sure about Nashville because he had been feeling less sure about us. I'm so glad we were on the phone and not on FaceTime, because I'm sure my face gave away my sinking spirit. I was terrified. But I listened.

He continued saying things like, *I'm not 100% sure our lives are headed in the same direction. I don't know yet what I want to do, and I don't know where that will lead me, and so I can't know if that aligns with what you want to do, and where you are being led and blah blah blah,* that tunnel vision thing was kicking in like the day Dustin left. I could hear sounds coming out, but couldn't make out the words. I watched the raindrops slide off the roof, plop down on the big hosta plant, hesitate for a second, and then roll down the edge of the leaf disappearing down into the grass. It was raining in slow motion. I kept the rocking chair rhythm at a steady pace, despite my insides wanting to scream out in pain.

Please God, don't take this from me.

I closed my eyes again, as we sat in silence for a good five minutes. I tried to respond, but I had trouble finding the words and didn't want to sound desperate or defensive. The silence confirmed that the winds were shifting, and I was afraid of which sail I would be turning to catch it.

We both knew this wouldn't be resolved in one phone conversation. We agreed to sleep on it and talk more tomorrow, and then awkwardly hung up. I kept rocking on the porch, and kept my phone up at my ear for several minutes after the call ended, like I didn't want to step into those changing winds just yet. I wanted to stay hovering in this weird moment where I could still taste the sweet parts of our relationship, and the bitter parts weren't quite there yet. It was the start of the car crash, and I didn't want to look away.

God, show me why I'm here, why I've been through what I've been through, and why Will is standing next to me now. Please do not take this away from me. I can't bear this burden again.

I stayed up most of the night praying and writing and reading and praying some more. My plane left the next morning, and I spent the flight from Portland to Minneapolis writing what I considered to be my last ditch effort to get him to stay. Not a conversation I ever expected just two days prior.

I called him up and read my plea to him, word for word from the Notes app on my phone, sitting on the floor at the Minneapolis airport. Tears streamed down my face, as I prayed he would hear me.

No discipline seems pleasant at the time, but painful. Later on, however, it produces a harvest of righteousness and peace for those who have been trained by it.

HEBREWS 12:11 (NLT)

He didn't hear me, I could tell it in his voice. Before we got off the phone, and after some more uncomfortable silence, I told him I felt like this relationship was slipping through my fingers like sand. What I wanted him to say was, *No, Kels, we'll figure this out. It's just a speed bump. It's going to be okay.*

What he actually said was nothing. Silence on the other end, while I waited patiently for reassurance I wasn't going to get.

We had a connection that was suddenly being severed, but there were still a few straggling strings attached, holding it all together. We could choose to repair it, or we could choose to amputate — cut it clean off. I was trying to do one, and the grieving really began in this moment, sitting on the floor at the airport, when I realized Will was trying to do the other.

Spotify kicked back on in my headphones as the call ended, and I walked to the bathroom near my gate. The song *Slip* by Elliot Moss came through my earbuds, and I rolled my eyes. *You gotta hold on, or it's gonna slip through your hands,* the lyric says. Loud and clear. I sobbed in the privacy of my bathroom stall, remembering two years earlier when I sat sobbing in another bathroom as my world crumbled around me. *How would I tell people? How would I explain it? How would I recover and move on? How long would that take? Who would replace him? What would people say?*

I boarded my connecting flight, and by the time I landed in Nashville, I had read nearly the entire book of Job, and I scribbled one of the last verses on a notecard when I got home: "Bear with me a little longer and I will show you that there is more to be said in God's behalf." Job 36:2 (NIV).

————

I count October 21st as the start of our relationship beyond friendship. So by those calculations, Will and I dated for 89 days.

Sometime around midnight the night I got home from Portland, Will finally broke up with me. After more unbearable silence and a reluctant, *Will, just say what's on your mind please,* he finally came out with it. *I think we should end it.*

He claimed his heart was no longer in it. I asked if that meant he wasn't ready or he wasn't interested. He said both. *Ouch.*

And so. many. long. pauses. It was torturous. Neither of us knew how to end the FaceTime. I finally broke the silence, and said I should go. His last send off was *Take care, Kelsey.* And I said, *You, too.*

So that's it? All those marriage talks and life planning conversations led up a take care *and a* you, too? *All those abandonment insecurities came true? My fears of him losing interest came true? What gives, God? Why are you doing this to me? I was so certain for so long about him. I felt like I was given sign after sign that he was it. That all that turmoil with Dustin was leading me straight to Will. I felt that so strongly in my gut. How can I ever trust that again? How can I know what is God's voice and what is my own?*

If I've prayed it once, I've prayed it a thousand times: *God, please let it be clear.*

———

The funny thing about grief is that it gets pegged as a stereotype — the feeling you get when something or someone dies. That's how most people think of it. But really, grief is the pain that ensues when anything important ends — a person's life, a relationship, a way you think your life will go.

In the weeks and months after that most awkward FaceTime breakup, I struggled with dozens of questions. *How did nine years of interest and four months of dating end suddenly within 48 hours, without much of an explanation? It took him over a month to get enough green lights to just ask me to be his girlfriend, so how did its undoing happen so quickly?*

I found myself back in the grieving process again, going through the five stages one at a time. These five stages were coined by Elizabeth Kübler-Ross way back in 1969: denial, anger, bargaining, depression, and acceptance.

First, *denial*. Oh boy, did I try to deny it. From that first moment that Will told me he was interested in me, I swear I felt such distinct clarity like I had never experienced before. It's like I had been in this musty, dimly lit room for the last couple years, trying to feel my way around and hope I didn't knock anything over. And when Will told me his real feelings about me, it was like someone finally flipped on the lights. *Of course! It's Will!* He's been right here in front of me all these years, and I just happened to already be tangled up with someone else. For the months we dated, I felt confirmation after confirmation that this relationship was right. That the Lord had led me through a failed marriage with Dustin in order to have a successful one with Will. I had begged the Lord to send me a helper, and he had dropped Will in my lap, and that was that. I was convinced this was my next chapter, so when Will rewrote the ending, I couldn't accept it.

Which leads me to *anger*. Good Lord, I was angry. Angry at him for talking about wedding rings, and then ending it just a few weeks later. I felt led on, and it was unbelievably irritating. I was angry at myself for falling in love with a guy that fell out of love with me — not once, but twice. I was angry at God for allowing me to go through this AGAIN. But most of all, angry that my judgement had been so off. Angry that my discernment of God's voice was telling me everything was falling neatly into place — when it was actually about to hit the fan.

I felt completely foolish, especially for being so damn sure. I had had so many great conversations with friends about what the Lord was doing in my life, and this great man he had brought into the picture. They shared in my joy then, and now I have to go back with my tail tucked and say *nope, I was wrong.* The humiliating part is that I've done that before. Two years earlier I had this same conversation with all these people, and the embarrassment was all too familiar. How foolish of me for thinking I understood what God was doing; for believing I was getting my life back, when it just came crumbling back down around me — again.

And so I *bargained.* I begged God to redeem our ending, and even tried desperately to keep lines open with Will for the same purpose. *Please, can we start again? It'll be different this time, we'll go slower, be more cautious. We'll get it right this time, I promise.* I prayed that our story wasn't over yet, and that God was brewing something for us just under the surface. Well, I wasn't completely wrong — He was definitely brewing something, it just had nothing to do with Will.

Next came the *depression.* Or better, there was always the depression. Not the clinically-diagnosed kind, but the sad, mopey, breakup kind. The kind of sadness that doesn't really go away with a funny movie or a pint of ice cream. It sets up camp in your heart, and stays for awhile. It plays *Pop Up Video* in your brain, reminding you of every little detail to be missed. It seeps into everyday life, and it's hard to shake. It's isolating, often crippling. This heavy sadness

MY TOP 6 THINGS *NOT* TO SAY TO
SOMEONE AFTER A DIFFICULT BREAKUP

1. Someone better will come along. Maybe that's true, but I kinda wanted *that* one. I had a thing going with *that* one.

2. Their loss. No actually, it's my loss, too. There were reasons we were together. It went two ways. The feelings, the love, the admiration — it was reciprocated. And so was the loss.

3. It wasn't meant to be. Where's the line between fighting for what you want and throwing in the towel too soon? And what do you do with all the confusion that's left over in the aftermath? It was a storm. There is debris. How do we clean up?

4. Everything happens for a reason. This is downplaying my pain, and it makes me feel like my struggle isn't worthy of being wrestled with. It's saying *everyone deals with crap, so learn to deal with your crap.* When all a grieving person really wants is for someone to sit with them in it.

5. He was a loser anyway. You deserve better. Wow, did you think that the whole time? Why didn't you ever speak up? Share your concerns in love and with respect, but don't wait until the heartbreak to do so.

6. You're too good for him. What can sound like a compliment can easily turn into an insecurity in the next relationship. Should I downplay my success to keep the next one around? Should I choose not to mention that great thing that happened, just in case it scares him away?

over the loss of Will stayed with me for nearly a year or more, and still finds its way into random moments even today.

And that's the stuff my therapist, Liz, taught me to sit in. Sit in the sadness. Don't shove it away or deny it it's place. Feel every ounce of it. A couple months later I would put this into practice when Dustin was in town for a day and took Poppy for me. I had an entire day kid-free, which hadn't happened in about eight months, so what did I do? I laid in bed and watched Netflix. All. Day. Long. It was a glorious and much needed break. I did nothing else. Except one moment when I thought of Will. And how I wished he was there with me for the day. I sat down in my closet when it hit me, and I decided to just sit in the sadness. I sobbed. I sobbed hard. I heaved over what I lost with him. I wept without abandon as I thought about his friendship and support. My sides hurt, my eyes hurt, my head hurt. My heart hurt most of all. I sat there a bit longer letting the wave die down. Then I stood up, wiped my tears on dirty laundry, and went back to my day. Liz was right — grieving leads to healing, and healing is living. I felt more alive and aware. I felt just a tad bit lighter.

But even with those heavy moments that come when I remember what was lost with him, and the realization that one life is slipping away and a new one is emerging — with all of that, *acceptance* starts to bloom. It's not necessarily a place you arrive at one day, it's an ongoing process that you're constantly working towards. You're learning to accept that you moved too fast with him. You're learning to accept that your expectations were unrealistic and too concrete for all the variables that get thrown into a dating relationship. Over time, the acceptance of that ending leads to the embracing of new beginnings. The pain dulls out, you don't think about him as much, and you finally move on. And you carry the lessons you learned with you into the next chapter.

In the span of four months, Will changed my life. Dramatic, but true. He challenged my relationship with God, and he encouraged me to form habits and practices that I never had before, but always knew I needed. He was the last straw in encouraging me to start counseling, which I am so grateful to have been in for that season. He helped change my perspective on what a godly relationship should look like, and more clarity on why my marriage with Dustin had ended. He was always quick to support and direct me back to God when I was struggling, and for that I am so thankful.

Will and I crossed paths not to be husband and wife, but to teach each other something else. He was the best possible first post-divorce boyfriend — not a catchy title, I know, but one he earned. He was kind, understanding, gentle, sympathetic, and generous. He knew my story, he loved my child, and he even loved me for a brief period. *Thanks for that, Lord. I see it now.*

———

Grief is an emotion I never paid much attention to, until it was staring me in the face. It stared me in the face as I mourned the loss of my marriage. It stared me down as I mourned the end of the story I had written for myself, and stepped into the new one that was unfolding in front of me. It snuck back in when I closed the laptop on Will that last night together. And grief continues to wiggle it's way in in new ways. It shows up at milestones, meltdowns, and memories that are supposed to have two people in them.

> Grief is an ongoing byproduct of an experience you can't shake. It's the wave that keeps crashing into the shore — sometimes violently, sometimes subtly.

Grief comes in stages, that stereotype is true, but it doesn't end with step five, Acceptance. Grief is an ongoing byproduct of an experience you can't shake. It's the wave that keeps crashing into the shore — sometimes violently, sometimes subtly. After you're tossed around a few times, you start to get the rhythm of the water, and you can recover from the crash more quickly. And slowly over time, you learn to channel your grief into other, more positive responses. Gratitude. Perseverance. Surrender. Even joy.

Years after Elizabeth Kübler-Ross penned her five stages of grief, her colleague and later co-author David Kessler argued that maybe there was a sixth stage: *meaning*. The belief that even after you accept the change, it becomes a part of your story — it serves a purpose. It's a thread that gets woven into your chapters and your seasons. It gets knotted up with other parts, becoming more noticeable at times, and fading back again later.

Grief is always there, but it doesn't have to show itself as the sadness it's often associated with. I much prefer redirecting my grief into gratefulness. And this is not an overnight switch. It's a constant, conscious choice you have to make when that beast rears its head. It's a decision to be grateful in the exact moment you find yourself in, rather than commiserate with the grief that will only pull you back into its lair. Don't let it take you there. Give it its 15 minutes, maybe, but channel the pain into something greater.

We're not pretending like it's not there — cause oh, honey, it's there — we're choosing to not let it control us. We're choosing gratitude over grief. Joy over mourning.

Ann Voskamp, author of *One Thousand Gifts*, wrote it on Facebook more eloquently than I could ever put it, and it just so happened to be on my wedding day — seven years after he said "I do" and just a couple years after he said "I don't."

> *So, if we're being honest here, maybe the work gave us a bit of grief today, and maybe the kids gave us some grief, Lord, and maybe we'll be bold enough and just say it out loud: we grieve a bit about how the day turned out, and how life's turned out, and how we've lost people we love, lost some dreams, lost hope of real change — in us, in our people, in the way things have gone. It's okay: The grief is simply proof that you're invested in living and loving. Grief is the guaranteed price we pay for love. And in the grief and paying that price, there's this enfolding comfort — of knowing we are spending our lives on the best things. And grieving how plans change — is part of Your plan to change us.*

So if you're having trouble seeing anything to be grateful for in the midst of your own grief, you can be grateful, at the very least, that you're spending your life on the best things — living and loving.

CHAPTER SIX

THE MOVE (AGAIN)

We will change in ways that we never imagined, and even though there is grief to leaving behind that old story, there is freedom and life and space waiting on the other side of the threshold.

SARAH BESSEY

You know when you're sick, and you've been in bed for days eating nothing but crackers and cough drops. But one evening, you're feeling a second wind, and you're thinking *maybe I'm on the mend.* So you muster up the energy to make yourself a real meal. But a few bites in, you realize it was all too much, too soon, and the next thing you know, you're puking up tacos, and then you can't ever eat tacos again. And it wasn't the tacos' fault — you were sick all along. The tacos were just bad timing.

That's what it was like when I moved from Missouri to Nashville, and then decided to move back just 10 months later.

It was all too much, too soon — the divorce, the pregnancy, the parenting, the business, the boyfriend — so maybe the decision to build an entirely new life in a new city probably *wasn't* the best

> [God] is not in such a hurry to give more light on the future than we need for action in the present, or to guide us more than one step at a time. When action is needed, light will come.
>
> J.I. PACKER

timing? Let me answer that one myself: It was *terrible* timing.

It wasn't Nashville's fault — I was sick all along.

Not physically sick, but I was sick of all the New. Learning to be single again was still new. Learning to be a mother was, for sure, new. Learning to parent without a partner was new. Learning to manage my online business was new — I had only quit my job and taken on freelance designing full-time for four months prior when I made the move. Learning to date again after the divorce was still new — learning to date, period, as an adult *still* feels New with a capital N.

So much of my life was new to me in the 18 months before the move that it was no wonder Nashville was just the guac that broke the taco's shell. My brain physically couldn't handle another New Thing, as badly as I wanted this fresh guac start to work.

And that loss of capacity for *new* stuff manifested itself in all the *familiar* stuff — the only familiar thing I had in Nashville, my family.

As much as my stubbornness doesn't want to type this on a screen and print this in a book, I was not a happy camper to be around those last few months in Nashville.

My mom and I particularly struggled a lot, and living together only amplified that wedge that was coming between us. *Be nice to your mother,* she half-jokingly said recently when I was giving her updates on this book. We can acknowledge now, years later, that we both said some things we wish we could take back. I know that season was one of the hardest for both of us. I know that she worried about me a lot. And I know she worried about me because she is my mother. If I were my mother, I would have worried about me, too. I was faced with a ton of new experiences that I had never encountered before — new city, new friends, changes in my business, and now a new relationship with someone she didn't really know very well. I understood her anxiety about it all, but I begged her to trust me. I was learning, I was growing, I was trusting in the Lord myself with all this, and the only thing I really knew to say was just to ask her to trust in Him, too.

———

After the first few weeks of counseling with Liz, I realized a recurring theme running through all of our conversations — I was bad at making decisions. Okay, maybe that's a little dramatic, but during this season of intense choices and huge life-changes — divorce decisions and pregnancy decisions and baby decisions and boyfriend decisions — I was struggling to find myself in all of it and make choices based on what *I* needed.

I was in damage control for a lot of years, reacting to what was happening around me. I was gathering up pieces from a shattered marriage, and trying to carry it into my new relationship with Will. I was gathering up the bits of motherhood that I had imagined for myself, and trying to reconcile it with the way my motherhood actually looked. I was on the defense, rarely making a decision that felt proactive, and just for *me*.

It all came to a head after a few months in Nashville, as I wondered if I was forcing my life to work in a place where I wasn't truly happy. My family and I made this decision to move together, but we moved with the acknowledgement that if it wasn't working out, we could just move back. In retrospect, we all knew Edit > Undo was an option, but we never considered what would happen if just *one* of us took the shortcut home.

I was coming to a crossroads where I couldn't please everyone. I wanted to be with my family, but this move was proving to be way harder than I expected. And with all the newness in my life that felt out of my control, where I lived was suddenly the only thing I *could* control. And any guilt about that looming decision was my own burden. Because feeling guilty implies that I've done something wrong. But I had done nothing wrong; I was just learning to make decisions for myself — hard decisions — and it honestly felt really selfish.

Liz talked about this spectrum that runs between selfishness (or even narcissism) and self*less*ness. On the selfish end, your decisions center around yourself without regard for others. On the other end, there's selflessness, and those decisions can be solely based on the opinions of others. The middle is where you want to be — that's where it's healthy. But most of us lean one way or another depending on our personality. For me, the chronic people pleaser, I lean towards the selfless side, but not always in the warm fuzzy way. Selflessness can also look a lot like cowering or shrinking back to avoid conflict and not ruffle feathers. In the same way, selfishness can sound all bad, but in fact it can look a lot like independence, confidence, and even freedom.

The hard part about all this, and the reason Liz was sharing it with me, is that no matter where you find yourself on the spectrum, any movement in the opposite direction of your natural tendency can feel like a giant leap. In one small step from making decisions for other people towards making

I was gathering up the bits of motherhood that I had imagined for myself, and trying to reconcile it with the way my motherhood actually looked.

decisions for yourself, it can feel like you're zooming to the other end of the spectrum at full speed. When in reality, it's just a step. There's tension, because the step is not in the direction you're used to going, but it's still just a step.

What I loved about Liz was that she would always direct the decision-making back to me — what do *I* feel and what do *I* think and what do *I* need. It felt selfish to want to move home, because that required leaving my family behind. Even knowing that it was what I *needed*, not just what I *wanted*. It felt like a giant leap towards selfishness, and I was convinced I was well on my way to full-on narcissism.

But it was just a step. A step towards independence, followed by confidence that I was making the right decision, and ultimately the freedom to step into the life that Poppy and I actually needed all along.

———

I was driving home from church one Sunday morning, and as I exited onto Highway 396 just outside of Nashville, I felt the Lord whisper to me — *I have big plans for you, and they're not necessarily in Tennessee.* It was a couple weeks after the breakup, and my heart was still fragile. I was still struggling to decipher the Lord's voice from my own voice, so whose was this? Was it just my exhausted subconscious telling me to give up and go back home? Or was I really hearing an answer? But it kept gnawing at me, as I glanced in the rearview mirror at Poppy sleeping peacefully. *Not in Tennessee.* Despite my doubts and insecurities in the promises I had been given, this little lift of the curtain reminded me to keep trusting. Keep moving forward, one foot in front of the other, and see where the Lord was leading this hot mess.

And so just seven months after moving to Nashville, I decided to move back home. That's a loaded sentence, because it was not a decision I came to quickly or easily. After countless pros-cons lists, and a million Thursday nights in Liz's office talking through the guilt and shame I felt for leaving my family, I boiled it down to three main reasons that I needed to go home. And because I'm a weirdo, I made them all start with F.

Number one, and probably most importantly — *familiarity.* I had gone through more life changes in the last two years than most people should go through in a decade. Sometimes I pinch myself and wonder if this is actually my life. It's the complete opposite of anything I ever expected. By the time I rolled into Nashville, I was freshly divorced, learning how to be a mom, still learning how to be single again, dipping my toes into dating, and adjusting to big, new changes in my business. As my dad so poignantly says, I had a lot of balls in the air. And throwing in a New City, Make All New Friends ball, was one too many balls to keep in my juggling act.

Poppy is screaming in the other room because she hasn't napped in two days. And I'm sick of it. And I feel like a terrible mom for saying that. I feel like a terrible mom a lot of the time.

Because I'm working when I should probably be playing with her. Because I lose my patience with her too often. Because sometimes, frankly, I don't enjoy any of it, and I miss the days when it was just me. Because I do this job alone, and it's so overwhelming that it's hard to be grateful for any of it. Because when people say how cute she is and how it must be so great being her mom, I just want to burst into tears and yell at them: it's so. damn. hard. you have no idea.

I hate living in Nashville. I feel so out of place here. I hate spending half my life in my car, driving 45 minutes to get anywhere. I hate not knowing where anything is. I hate relying on a map to get me absolutely anywhere. I hate getting lost. I hate constantly being the new person. I'm sick of trying to make friends. I'm sick of feeling like I'm missing something, because apparently everyone else here just loves Music City. I miss being around people who actually know me. I miss being around people I don't have to try with.

It's all exhausting and stressful, and I just want to go home. And Poppy's still crying.

So they started dropping, rolling away, slipping out of my grip. There was nothing familiar in my life anymore. It was all new, and frankly, it was all hard. I craved anything recognizable. When I would go back to Missouri for holidays, I dreaded driving back to Tennessee at the end of the trip. I dreaded going back to the never-ending Google maps, the insecurities of always being the new girl, and the constant search for a new doctor, mechanic, dentist, eye doctor, dog groomer, all of it. It was too much, too soon. There were too many balls in the air, and I had to take some out of the game. I finally realized that in order to focus on all the new, I had to plant myself in the familiar. There was only one new thing that I could control, and that was where I chose to live.

The second reason was *freedom* — namely and a little ironically, freedom from my own child. If you're not a parent and you're gasping at this, just you wait. Cause all the parents are reading this and nodding their heads vigorously. Parents need breaks from their children. There, I said it.

Sweet, sweet Penelope. I love you, darling, but I desperately need breaks from you. As a single parent, you don't have a spouse to tap out with at 5:00. You're on, and you're alone, 100% of the time, morning to night. I giggle under my breath when I hear other moms panic because their husbands will be out of town for the weekend. Because that is all of my weekends. No mom-shaming or judgement — because yes, it is hard being a parent no matter what circumstance you're in — but seeing another perspective can sometimes shift your own.

In Nashville, I felt extremely isolated with Poppy. I worked from home with no childcare, except for a three hour stretch each week when my sister-in-law and I would trade kids for an afternoon. I lived with my mom, and while she was home a lot in the first couple months while she job hunted, all moms know that even when someone else is watching your kid in your own house, you're never fully off the clock. And once she started her full-time job, it was back to me and Poppy and two wild dogs who did a lot of barking. I didn't have other friends or family that could babysit for quick errands or appointments, and so I often felt trapped in my own house.

I couldn't afford to put Poppy in daycare, and every time I considered it, the research of finding the right one would give me analysis paralysis. It didn't take long to remember and miss the community of people I had left behind in Springfield who were helping me with Poppy. And while a handful of that community had come with me to Nashville, we each had our own lives and responsibilities, and it frankly wasn't enough help for me.

Single parenting takes a village, and I had moved out of my village. And it was

> I'll show up and take care of you as I promised and bring you back home. I know what I'm doing. I have it all planned out — plans to take care of you, not abandon you, plans to give you the future you hope for.
>
> JEREMIAH 29:10-11 (MSG)

maybe the hardest reality to realize that even Poppy's dad was part of that village. The most valuable person to provide the freedom I craved was the one person I did not want to admit that I needed. But being back home would mean Dustin would have her more often and for longer. Consistent, overnight breaks would help me keep my sanity, but it seemed like a far off dream. The longer I went without those breaks, the more I could tell my stress level went up, my patience went way down, and I just wasn't enjoying my own child. And I hated that feeling most of all, not to mention the guilt that came with it.

I needed more freedom with Poppy in order to be the kind of mother I wanted to be, and the kind of mother she needed me to be. And despite the bitterness and resentment I still harbored for Dustin, I knew that Poppy needed to have a relationship with her dad, and my freedom as a single mother could only come from his help. As I come from a long line of stubborn women, that was a hard thing to admit.

My last reason for moving back home was *finances*. I went from dirt-cheap Missouri to up-and-coming Nashville, and my bank account couldn't keep up. My business was shifting a lot during this season, and while I had honestly made more money in my five months in Music City than I had from my entire annual salary at my old job, I was still pouring way more money than I was used to into everyday bills and expenses. My rent in Nashville (even with my mom as a roommate) was nearly double what my mortgage was in Missouri. My mom and I lived five suburbs removed from actual Nashville in order to afford the size place we needed. Because of that, I did way more driving and commuting and sitting in traffic for up to an hour just to get to my basic places like church or the grocery store. I felt like half my brain power was used up figuring out where things were, how far away they were, how long it would take to get there, and blah blah blah. Every time I left my house, I felt like I was going on a road trip. And these were not the types of things I wanted to be spending my time, money, or energy on.

As with any good Type A planner who likes to weigh all the options over and over and over again, I ran the numbers on what it would take for me and Poppy to stay in Nashville and get our own place. I started looking at houses online and dreaming of what it would be like to stick it out here, and try to make this work. If I stayed, I wanted to be in a more populated area, not five suburbs away from the city. I found this adorable house in Nashville city limits that was exactly what I was looking for. It was a little cottage that was eerily similar to my house I had just sold in Missouri. It had a stone chimney on the front, with ivy scattering along the cracks. It had two bedrooms and two bathrooms, just enough room for me and Poppy and our Cooper dog. It had a small yard, was in an average neighborhood, and I could envision us there. And then I looked at the price. This house was listed at around $425,000. Nearly half a million dollars. A far cry from the nearly identical house I had just sold in Missouri for a whopping $91,000.

That was my Oprah "aha moment." I sat back on my bed, closed my glowing laptop screen in the dark, and realized I couldn't afford to stay in Nashville even if I wanted to.

———

I don't doubt God brought me to Nashville for a reason. It stretched me, challenged me, made me stronger, and made me surrender my life completely to Him, even more than my divorce did. As I wrestled with this decision, worked my way past the burden I felt to stay put for my family's sake, and into the freedom of knowing I had to make this call for myself, the answer became clear.

Around that time my friend Amber sent me the song *Oceans* by Hillsong United, and encouraged me to listen to it on repeat. That was an easy choice to make, unlike all the others swirling around my head, and the lyrics quickly became my sustenance for the months that would follow:

Spirit lead me where my trust is without borders,
let me walk upon the waters, wherever you would call me.
Take me deeper than my feet could ever wander,
that my faith would be made stronger,
in the presence of my Savior.

This song sounds like the start of a fresh chapter, to trust God with a new beginning. But it spoke to me in a different way. Maybe God wasn't walking me into a new place, but maybe he was returning me back to an old place with fresh eyes. Bringing me back home, in order to make it new again. I think a lot about redemption in my story, and what it means for the Lord to *redeem* you. I heard a pastor once liken it to more modern uses of the word "redeem," as in, to redeem a coupon or a voucher. You're trading in one thing of value for another thing of value. The origin of the word comes from the Old Latin word "redimere." Literally, to "buy back."

I left Springfield during a season where every shop on every corner reminded me of a memory with Dustin. I couldn't drive by the Campbell 16 movie theater without remembering our first kiss there in high school. That park off Kimbrough where we got caught in the rain that one time. Avanzare is where we spent our last

Valentine's Day, over pasta and wine. Every inch of that town was littered with evidence of us, and it was a painful place to be.

I thought Nashville would be my redemption, but maybe it was just my waiting room. Maybe the Lord was letting me hit pause and escape a city of painful memories, in order to "buy me back." To redeem me at a future date; exchange the old for the new. Maybe the returning home was the redemption, not the leaving.

———

I've always wanted to buy an old house and fix it up, long before it was the plot line of every single HGTV show. I was drawn to the old, beat up gems with the creaky floors and the thick, intricate molding. The ones that had a story to tell, and made me wonder about the families that lived there long before its current residents. What celebrations did it hold, and what traumas did it live through? Old houses had character and scars, and though their bones were solid as a rock, they were broken in places. They had lived a lot of life, and it showed.

Maybe God wasn't walking me into a new place, but maybe he was returning me back to an old place with fresh eyes. Bringing me back home, in order to make it new again.

That's the kind of house I searched for when I started house hunting back in Missouri. My house hunting was all done online, and I only ever looked at two houses in person. One I put an offer on *after* I looked at it, and the second I looked at *after* I put an offer on it.

The first I'll call the Kings House, and it was beautiful. It was made of Carthage stone, had towering old trees, built-in nooks, and the best part — an attached greenhouse in the back. As soon as I opened up the greenhouse door, I could picture all of it: I was holding a cup of coffee, Cooper running out in front down the walkway, Poppy and her pigtails close behind checking on the sprouting plants in our little glass oasis. I imagined sitting out in the light-filled living room working, while Poppy played with a basket of toys on the wood floor. I could hear laughter of friends and family filling up the kitchen for dinner parties, and that loud but muddled sound you hear when four conversations are going on at once.

The scenes were so vivid in my mind, and I loved all of it. I was enjoying my own child, I was smiling, I felt satisfied and finally whole again. It was all so close, I could taste it.

The price tag on the Kings House was a little above my budget, and so I made my offer a few thousand under the asking price. They countered back with the same asking price — they wouldn't budge. My heart sank, knowing I didn't have any other prospects, except maybe this old white house on Fremont, but it needed more work than I could handle.

Right? It needed too much work, right? The kitchen was falling apart, there was no garage for my car, and I would need to fence the yard right away. It was too much work. The bathroom was pretty small, there was no dishwasher and no central air conditioning. Every time I'd sift through the photos of the Fremont House, I'd talk myself out of it, and move on to the dwindling list of homes in my budget and style. But I'd always find myself back at the Fremont House listing, thinking *maybe ...*

Surely there was something wrong with that house, it had been on the market for months without any takers. And it sat in a neighborhood where houses do not sit for sale like that. It's the adorable, historic, quaint center-city neighborhood you imagine with tree-lined streets, picket fences, and a local coffee shop just 60 seconds from the front porch steps. It was the street I drove down the night Dustin left, on my way to and from my mom's house, when I tucked a certain "old house" dream back into my pocket to focus on the other matters at hand — like that dang baby. It was literally the exact place I wanted to live. But it needed too much work.

And then I started watching this little TV show called *Fixer Upper*. Maybe you've heard of it? Chip and Jo showed me night after night how to shop for a house and account for renovations at the same time. With every episode I devoured, I thought *Yes, Chip! I can do this!*

I came back to the Fremont House listing one more time — the bones were there, it was my dream location, it was under budget with room for a reno budget, and so I called my friend and realtor, Missy, in Springfield. She had been eyeing the house, too, and agreed to go over for a walk-through with me on FaceTime. She met our other friend Adie there, and the two of them carried me around the house on the phone talking through their thoughts and concerns. I love these two ladies so much for that simple afternoon. It was a small thing for them, but it meant the world to have two trusted friends — and fellow old house owners — be my eyes and ears when I couldn't be there. They're in my village, for sure.

They checked door knobs, flushed toilets, listened for floor creaks, and tested faucets. There were no glaring issues besides a less than attractive, but functioning kitchen. And so I made my choice — with Liz in my head — to do this for myself. To give myself the freedom of a new old house in a new old place, so I could start over, *again*.

I put in my offer, we negotiated the price, and they confirmed that I was an old house loving buyer and not an investor that would let it be destroyed by cheap student renters. And so one week after my 28th birthday, I became the proud owner of an 84-year-old house that I had never actually stepped foot in.

I was learning to trust my gut again. Learning to make big decisions with one step towards being a little selfish for once. I was learning not to feel guilty for taking that step, and knowing that it was a step towards health. I could pour love into this old house, my sweet Poppy, and even myself again. I had been beaten up over the last two years, tossed from life change to life change, and coming home was such a sweet relief. I could breathe again; I could start over again. It was a step towards a redemption story that was quietly unfolding in front of me.

And a house can't breakup with you unexpectedly, right? Like, you're kind of stuck with each other for a while, right? I'm perfectly okay with that.

———

I bought my old white house on Fremont in March, and by the end of May I was following a moving truck back through western Tennessee, across the state line, through the boot heel of southeast Missouri, and back into the Ozarks. I had my now almost

MY TOP 9 THINGS TO FIX IN MY
VERY OLD HOUSE (AND SOME TO KEEP)

1. Rickety crystal door knobs that no, I will not replace.

2. No locks on the basement windows for the first 18 months of living there. Like, push them open easily with a light finger nudge, and come on in, Serial Killers.

3. A front door that sticks in the summer and lets the icy air right on in during the winter. And *every single* repairman comments on it.

4. The blackened underbelly of my fireplace mantel, from roaring fires of decades passed.

5. 90's boob lights. They were the first to go.

6. Crumbling shelves inside the kitchen cabinets. Any dishes besides paper or plastic were too heavy to live there.

7. The mysterious light switch on the backside of the house that turns on nothing. Just ... nothing.

8. The mysterious hallway light that has no light switch. (No, it's not the one outside.) Just unscrew the bulb to turn it off, or better yet, leave it on 24/7. Who needs light switches anyway?

9. Add a back door, cause those are usually good for safety and stuff like that, right?

two-year-old Poppy in the backseat keeping Cooper company who was anxiously riding in his crate next to her. My dad was behind the wheel of the U-haul truck up ahead, filled with all the same furniture and boxes I came to Nashville with just 10 months earlier.

It was after the long eight hour drive, when I came home to a house full of friends waiting to unload the moving truck and assemble countless pieces of furniture with tiny IKEA tools, that I knew I had made the right choice. There was something different about rolling into Springfield on that Friday evening in the pouring rain. It felt different than all the other times I had come over that hill on Highway 60 to see the first of many Springfield exits. This time it felt more like home than it ever had; it felt *right* and *good*.

And it was about a week after that, sitting around a table full of women that would soon become like family, that I knew for sure, for sure that coming home was exactly what I needed.

The table and the house belonged to Jenn, and the invitation to sit at it came from Shailey. I had known Shailey for several years, from church as well as working together on projects for the design agency I worked for around the time my life exploded. Shailey is the sweetest human being on planet Earth, and as I sat in her living room the weekend I was in town for my house inspection, she invited me to a girls' group she was a part of, hosted bi-weekly by the lovely Jenn who happened to live three streets over from my new old house.

Boxes were still piled around me that first week back home, but despite all the excuses I was coming up with, I forced my introverted self to go to my first girls' group night. It was basically the exact same scenario as the winter of my pregnancy, forcing me and my growing belly to go to a small group at church, among women that would soon become my village.

We sat outside in Jenn's gorgeous backyard at a table with perfectly mismatched chairs and cushions. I was nervous and anxious and exhausted from moving, but I tried my best to keep up with names and faces. But this was different than these same new person feelings in Nashville. I was in the town I had grown up in with women who had also lived here for years and years, so names and faces were often somewhat familiar. Hazards of a smaller town. Karen owned that coffee shop where my best friend's sister worked. Mara was already a designer I kept up with on Instagram. Those three went to high school with my brother. Katie somehow knows everyone I know, and we still can't figure out how we didn't meet sooner.

I had been beaten up over the last two years, tossed from life change to life change, and coming home was such a sweet relief. I could breathe again; I could start over again. It was a step towards a redemption story that was quietly unfolding in front of me.

We had a lot in common, and that was comforting, but there was also the glaring difference that I'm always annoyingly aware of — I was the only single parent. The only single person, period, actually. Everyone was either married or nearly there, and I was quick to notice it. Also probably the *only* one who noticed, because when you're divorced you feel like maybe it's tattooed on your forehead and it's all anyone is thinking about, but it's a tattoo only you are paying attention to.

That first girls' group was overwhelming and somehow calming at the same time. Like a nice big exhale after a long, labored breath in. I felt like I had finally found my people, and they had literally been in my backyard the whole time. The second girls' group was when I spilled my guts to them — woke up happily married one morning, and divorce-bound and pregnant by dinner time. I told them about moving to Nashville and back, and I told them aaaaall about Will. They cried with me, and laughed with me, and for the first time in a while, I felt seen. I had spilled my guts to new friends in Nashville a few times, and it never felt reciprocated. I had always felt like an emotional wreck with enough baggage for a family of 12 flying to Disney World. I would puke up my life story, and then quietly try to clean it up while they changed the subject to something lighter and easier to stomach.

But these girls welcomed the puke. They welcomed the baggage and the crying and the heartbreak I was carrying around with me. They let me dump it there in Jenn's living room, and nobody was afraid of it. Just like Liz, they held space for me. The group is still going strong today, and every other Tuesday night you can find us crying until we're hysterically laughing, or the other way around. But in those first few girls' groups, I was seen and heard and known among a group of women I had just met.

Yes, I was finally in the right place.

CHAPTER SEVEN

THE DATING

"Sometimes you don't even want to keep the person, you just want to keep the feeling of being loved and chosen at the end of a day."

HANNAH BRENCHER

A few months ago, my friend Amanda and I signed up to go to a speed dating event in town. It was by application only, and I almost didn't sign up. But what did I have to lose? So I applied, got in, and ran into several girlfriends in the week leading up to the event who had also signed up. Amanda and I were anxiously excited to just see what was out there.

So when we got the email that the event was cancelled, we were both pretty surprised. But then they gave their reason for cancelling it, and we were suddenly not surprised at all — no men had signed up. Of course. We laughed, went out for pizza instead, and maybe said some special words. Our sad reality had just been confirmed — there are quite literally zero men left.

Shoulda known.

This sadly funny turn of events basically sums up my dating life since Will and I broke up. It has now been over two years since that horribly awkward FaceTime call, and I have been on a grand total of … drum roll please … three and a half dates. *Wow, Kelsey! Way to get back out there!* I know, it's a staggering number. *Like, how did you even have time for all those dates? And also, how do you go on half a date?*

Let's start with the first two dates of the three and a half. These two were with a very nice guy I'll call Ken, because he reminded me of Barbie's man. He was tall, blonde, extremely polite, and might have been made of plastic. Ken and I were set up on a blind date by my friend Katie from the girls' group, who jokes that her mission in life is to find Poppy a step-dad. I appreciate her enthusiasm for this mission, because I have lost mine. (Katie, I know you're reading this, and you are the literal best.) She plopped us all in a group text message, made some hilarious introductions, and then kindly showed herself out. *What a time to be alive, right?*

Ken was kind and witty and creative and cute. He adored his family, and actually had a real job and a real car and a real dog that he took care of all by himself. He was checking off lots of boxes right away. But there was one big box that wasn't being checked — his faith. After the deep spiritual connection that Will and I had, that Dustin and I were trying to have but never did, I realized this was a deal breaker for me. I wanted my partner to share that piece of my life with me, and nothing against Ken in the slightest, but that just wasn't a part of his life. I quickly realized this missing piece, and so it was very hard to break the news to him at the end of the second date. He was a gentleman, he was extremely respectful of my decision, and I felt like the worst person on the planet.

I drove home from that second date in tears, partially because I was frustrated at this whole dating thing. Have I mentioned it sucks? It sucks. It's putting yourself out there, being vulnerable with a near-stranger, with no guarantee that they'll reciprocate or even care. I was frustrated with the process, and maybe more frustrated knowing that that was the only way through it.

But I also cried tears for Will, oddly enough. Though it was obviously a vastly different circumstance, I was the one doing the rejecting, and I had never been on that side of the equation. It was the *it's not you, it's me* conversation, and I ate some of my words from when Will was saying the same things to me. I went back to that season, during our breakup, and put myself in his shoes. I wept in my car knowing how hard that must have been for him, and it may have been that moment when I forgave him.

And as I type this now, I wonder why I didn't think of Dustin in the car that day. How hard it must have been for him to end a marriage — not just a relationship — with an explanation that even he had trouble putting into words. I don't know why I thought of Will's breakup, and not my divorce. Maybe it was the proximity, but I think it also had to do with forgiveness. Forgiving Dustin is something I'm still working on. It's a harder place to get to, and I'm seeing more and more that maybe it's not a place at all. Maybe it's a decision that I have to make daily to not hold all of this against him. To not blame him for the fact that Will came into my heart and then broke it. To not blame

> Wait patiently for the Lord. Be brave and courageous. Yes, wait patiently for the Lord.
>
> PSALM 27:14 (NLT)

him for all the hours I've wasted swiping through dating apps. To not blame him for having to sit across from this kind, gentle, put-together Ken doll and tell him *no* over a nice, Saturday brunch. To not blame him for the emotional drive home, and the frustration that I'm back at Square One. I can acknowledge how difficult that must have been for Dustin, but I can't forgive him just yet.

During my counseling with Liz in Nashville, this topic came up a few times, and she always reminded me that forgiveness is not for the other person, it's a kindness we give to ourselves. That makes it sound a little easier, but even extending ourselves that kindness can feel impossible. I'm a work in progress, here, as you can see.

This all sounds a bit dramatic for a two-date guy, but it opened my eyes to the other side for a bit. And for the record, neither side feels good. The rejection is hard, the reject*ing* is hard; it's a roller coaster that you just have to sit on until the end. And then you jump onto the next ride, buckle yourself in, and do it all over again.

What about online dating, Kelsey? I mean, it's 2018. Great question, reader friend. I had tried online dating for a few months upon moving to Nashville, and I went on one single date with a guy that I met on an app that shall remain nameless and rhymes with *hinder.* He was pre-Will, so I'm not counting him in my 3.5 dates, but just know that he was very nice, and he did not murder me. There was zero spark there, and all we really did was swap divorce stories over a cup of coffee at Frothy Monkey one Friday evening. To be honest, that whole online dating world was just *weird* to me. Dating is one thing, but online dating? It's so weird, you guys. Like *weird* weird. I totally understand that people meet and even get married that way all the time, and I have close friends to prove it, but for me, I just couldn't handle it. I watch too much *Dateline*, and I was convinced they were all going to murder me. Also, Facebook stalking just sort of ruins half the fun of getting to know a person, right?

So back in Missouri, post-Will, I was meeting up with my fellow single friend Ashley for dinner one night. Ashley and I were commiserating over tacos when we decided we had to be at least a *little* proactive with this whole dating thing. We made a pact that we would each try out the dating app Bumble for a month. It was an app where only the women could initiate conversations, not the men, and we were intrigued. I had tried other apps, but not Bumble, and Ashley had never tried any, so we figured it would be a fun experiment. We would commit to putting ourselves out there, and we would reconvene in a month with our results.

She met a man named Jesús who proved to be a bit of a stalker, and I met a nice guy named Chad who did not seem to be a stalker. Our bars were set pretty high, as you can see. Which brings me to the third of the inordinate three and a half dates. I'm 99.9% sure he'll never pick up this book, but just in case, I'll rename him Chad, because he just kind of seemed like a Chad, ya know?

Chad and I met up for drinks at a place down the street from my house, and it didn't take too many sips into my Riesling to see that we had zero things in common. I figured he would call it when our glasses were empty, but he surprisingly offered another round, and I surprisingly accepted. The more we talked, the more we just kept digging our graves. He was fixated on the fact that we went to rivaling high schools — *10 years ago*. He just couldn't shake it, poor guy. And when I asked him about his job that he hated, I couldn't get past the fact that he had no intentions of leaving it. The way he described his life sounded like there were few things he was passionate about or even proud of. Yet he had no desire to change his circumstances.

This baffled me on my walk home, and as I started getting ready for bed that night, I realized there was a really big box that was left off my imaginary list of qualifications for my imaginary partner. He needs to have some ambition, for goodness' sake. Chad was hanging out in his mediocre life (his words), and he didn't seem the least bit interested in improving himself in any way. Old Kelsey would have said, *oh, I can fix him*. But New Kelsey said, *add it to the list*.

Ambition is an interesting word — it's the one you see on inspirational posters and from motivational speakers. It one of those things they highlight in your last few months of high school, and then you never really hear about it again. But Chad reminded me that ambition is a huge deal even 10 years after high school — much more so than *which* high school you attended, dude. It's working towards something, trying to achieve something, making yourself better. This drive to improve comes naturally to me, but Chad showed me loud and clear that it does not come naturally to everyone.

And so dating can help you realize what you *don't* want. Your deal breakers, your *no thank you's*, your pass button. Playing it safe and choosing to stay mediocre, maybe that's on my deal breaker list — and maybe I like adventure more than I realized.

MY TOP 8 DEAL BREAKERS IN
YOUR ONLINE DATING PROFILE

1. Shirtless mirror selfies. Just, no. NO.

2. Photos with unexplained women. So, is that your sister orrrr ... your girlfriend?

3. Photos with clearly cropped out women. It doesn't take Sherlock to notice those lady hands draped around your shoulder.

4. Fuzzy photos. Come on, it's not 2006.

5. Vague profile description. When you list your interests as "hanging out with friends, going places, and doing fun stuff," that's just not helpful. That literally describes everyone on this weird little app.

6. No profile description. Let's show a *little* effort, maybe.

7. A job you probably shouldn't have when you're 32. Maybe just save the fast food cashiers for the high school kids, yeah?

8. Group photos. I've never met you, remember?

And when you've swiped so many times that it literally gets to the end of the men and says there's no one left, that's when you shut it down, Liz Lemon style. I'm embarrassed to admit how many times this has happened to me.

Which brings me to the *half* in three and a half dates. It wasn't a *half* because it was cut short, it was a *half* because it wasn't quite a date to begin with. It was with an old friend from grade school who I'll call James. James was the guy who was kind to everyone, no matter their circle of friends or popularity. He was witty, he was smart, and the thing I liked most was his deep rooted faith in God. And also, James was very nice to look at. (No shame.) But I really hadn't spoken to him in at least 10 years, and so I went out on a limb and did something I'd never done then or since — I asked *him* out on a date.

I sent off the message with sweaty palms and a racing heart. I definitely wasn't getting any kind of work done that day, and so I napped. And I had this dream:

I was on an airplane that was landing. There were no other seats or people on the plane, just me sitting right in the middle. But there was one flight attendant, and she was standing right in front of me, her hands on my shoulders, bracing me as we landed — as if I had no seat belt. The brakes weren't working or something went wrong, and suddenly we were sliding all over the runway. My laptop was on the tray over my lap, but it started sliding off. The flight attendant was still there holding on to me, as I tried to hold on to everything on my tray. The plane finally came to a stop, and the flight attendant was still standing in front of me, hands on my shoulders, unmoved. I never looked up or saw her face. I just took off my glasses and started crying into my hands. I felt so incredibly alone, except for this flight attendant still gripping my shoulders.

And then I woke up (and feverishly wrote it all down). The dream was vivid and so real. There must be meaning in there somewhere — I was literally sitting in the middle, alone. *Was the landing that 180 seconds of fear? The 3 minutes between the wheels coming out and touching the ground when it all just feels a little shaky? Who was the flight attendant? And why didn't she ever let go of me?*

I had a lot of questions — and still do — but there was a replied message waiting on my phone from James. Being the incredibly kind and gracious guy he is, he politely declined an official "date," noting that he had just come out of a relationship where he was engaged. Cue my huge face palm. But he did agree to a cup of coffee and catching up. *What the heck,* I thought, *nothing to lose.*

So it wasn't quite a date, but I'll count it as half. Our half date was fine. Ugh, it was fine. Can you tell how over this dating thing I am? He was exactly how I remembered him: kind, gracious, polite, soft-spoken, a little mysterious, a little goofy. We talked about our careers — he had some very clear ambitions, take notes Chad — our families, and our past relationships. There were so many similarities in this relationship he had just come out of and mine with Will that still felt fresh, even though it had been over a year. We sympathized on that weird fog that you find yourself in following a breakup. You're not really sure what just happened or how you feel about it or where you'll go next. The dust is still settling, and you can't quite see in front of you yet. You're waiting and rehashing and running through all the what-ifs. A little like the fog you feel when you wake up from a vivid dream that you can't sort out.

It's not a fun place to be in, but having been in that exact spot a year prior, I understood exactly what he was going through, and so we just left things there with our half-date and our empty coffee mugs. I drove home frustrated. Yet again. Rejection is hard, even if just for obvious reasons like timing. I laid my cards on the table, but they weren't picked up. It's easy to go to the selfish place of wondering what pieces of you aren't good enough. Not pretty enough, not smart enough, not spiritual enough? Or even what pieces of you are too much. Too independent? Too much baggage? One too many ex-husbands?

It's easy to go selfish when a situation doesn't go our way, rehashing ways we could have played our hand differently. But the reality is, maybe the other person is just playing an entirely different game. They've got their own set of cards that they're struggling to figure out how to play, and it has nothing to do with your hand. One of you is about to yell *Uno*, and the other is getting sandbag after sandbag in Spades. It's nobody's shortcomings that make the game unplayable, it's just that we haven't quite found the person who's playing the same game we are. And most people are just doing their best with what they have in front of them. It's not very encouraging when you're sitting across the table from these very-nice-to-look-at people, but it can at least lend us some perspective when we find ourselves being the one to say *no*. And it's kind of the entire process of dating.

Whether or not you're in the dating scene, you don't have to look far to see relationships around you crumble because they were playing different games. I recently watched my dad go through this with a 15-year relationship he was in. You'd think after 15 years, they'd be playing the same game, but sadly they weren't. Hearts were broken, wounds were ripped open, and it was an ending none of us saw coming. It's one thing to go through this type of sudden, pain-riddled breakup yourself, but it can be a whole other beast to witness someone close to you go through it, too. You know the deep, unshakable pain it brought you, and your heart bleeds for your loved one now feeling the same. It breaks your trust in the person who inflicted the pain, and the entire dating system itself. It plants

It's easy to go selfish when a situation doesn't go our way, rehashing ways we could have played our hand differently. But the reality is, maybe the other person is just playing an entirely different game.

yet another seed of fear that everyone walks away at some point — you *will* be abandoned sooner or later. And it makes it that much harder for the next person to see the real you.

It doesn't take a thousand dates to know that dating is not easy. Three and half will do the trick. Yeah, there are the fun outings, getting dressed up, washing your hair (I should probably do that more anyway). But a lot of people don't talk about the ugly side — the uncertainty and the unknown, the difficult conversations, the fear of it all ending in an instant, and then the heartbreak when it does.

And the frustrating thing is, I don't have an answer for this. I don't have a remedy that wraps this dating chapter up nicely with a bow. I'm still in the trenches of this battle myself. I'm still trying to find my way, my person. I'm still figuring out how I'll explain all these fears and insecurities to someone someday, and it can be hard to imagine them choosing to stay at my table rather than turning to the one nearby to play a different game. But I'm trusting God with these fears. I'm remembering that He can see the whole painting, and I can just see a few little strokes. I don't question that everything I've gone through has led me to this place, but it's hard to see the value in the pain when you can't see exactly where it's leading you next.

———

When you're in the dating world, no matter your age or circumstance, it can feel like you're constantly hitting a wall. You ride this cruel rollercoaster of ups and downs — the high of meeting someone new and feeling hopeful, the low of realizing he's not it, and the high of meeting the next person. And sometimes the roller coaster tracks get twisted together — you're still sitting in the low of a relationship that ended, but feeling optimistic with this new guy sitting across from you. But why can't you shake the thought of the last one?

Stephanie May Wilson, a writer for single women, shifted my perspective once with one simple sentence in one of her email newsletters: "None of them are supposed to work out, except one." That forces you to have a pretty low batting average (look Dad, a baseball reference!), and in turn, that drastically lowers your great expectations. Not the expectation of what I'm looking for — that bar is set high thanks to all the no's that will come before him.

The expectation that's lowered is the one that says all these first dates and second dates should be knocking it out of the park every time. (Dad! More baseball!) Very few of them will even come close to knocking it out of the park. Some will get close, and you'll have that slow-motion moment before the ball drops onto the outfield when you realize it wasn't a home run. And then you'll just jog back to the dugout and wait for the next one. Theoretically, you'll only get one home run in this entire game.

And I know that's both weirdly encouraging and stupidly discouraging, and enough with the baseball metaphors, Kelsey.

So what do you do while you're waiting for the home run? The interim is a weird stretch of time, and if that's where you find yourself, know that I am right there with you shrugging my shoulders, too. The waiting period, the in-between, it's not a place you pay much attention to until you're there. You can't go back and change what was, but you can't quite go forward yet either. It's a stuck feeling.

But I have good news. You don't have to feel stuck all the time. Yes, you will most certainly feel stuck home alone on a Saturday night eating cereal for dinner, folding laundry, and trying to figure out why you're still watching *Scandal* after all those ridiculous plot twists. You will feel stuck and sad and confused on those nights. Partially because of *Scandal*, but mostly because you don't have a partner to share the little things with.

But those nights will become fewer and farther between if you can channel this season into something good. Don't wallow; get out of the house. Even with the tinge of grief that lingers around like a creeper, you can still be content — no, *thrive* — in your singleness. This is your chance to do things and try things while your schedule is freed up. Don't look at your calendar and think of all the dates you're missing out on; think of the things you can fill it up with.

For example, travel. I've taken some of the most amazing trips of my life while I've been single. It's easy to think that you can't travel because you don't have anyone to go with — false, friend. Chances are you have good friends that have moved away — go see them.

Chances are you have girlfriends who are itching to get out of town — scratch their itch. Siblings make awesome travel partners because you have a lifetime of inside jokes just waiting to be revived. My brother, Taylor, and I have taken several trips together, and they're some of my favorites. We've eaten at world-renowned restaurants that were on our bucket lists, we've practiced our worst Italian accents over bowls and bowls of life-changing pasta, we've made fun of each other all over Europe. And then there's your parents. Whose mom wouldn't cry at the invitation to join you on a good old-fashioned road trip? Mine for sure would be in tears. Whose dad wouldn't beam during a Friday night date with his daughter? Mine does, often over a plate of sushi.

> If all I know of harvest,
> is that it's worth my
> patience, then if You're
> not done working, God
> I'm not done waiting.
>
> SEASONS, HILLSONG WORSHIP

I'm convinced that traveling with the people you love is the best way to show the real you. And even traveling alone can be a nice change of pace — you get to pick where you want to eat, and you don't have to worry about anyone else's feelings. That's a relief, huh? Can you tell I like food a lot?

Single parenting isn't all hard, because frankly, it makes travel way easier. I have a built-in babysitter who is just as capable with Poppy as I am — her dad. And he is the one person that I will never, ever travel with. Dramatic, but true. I get a couple full days off a week from parenting, and I need those days off to survive the other five on my own. And sometimes I take those days to get away, so I'm even more refreshed when that pigtailed girl comes running back into my arms. Self-care. It's a real thing, and it's a necessary thing — no matter who you are.

If traveling isn't in the budget, just shoot for a cup of coffee. I've been making it a point to get together with one of my girlfriends at least once a week. We all know those conversations — *It's been forever! We should hang out! Totally, I'll look at my calendar!* You never look at your calendar, you never hang out, and you have the exact same conversation a year later in the frozen aisle at Walmart. I'm guilty of it, too, so don't feel bad. But in your singleness, be intentional about these friendships. Go through your social media account and make an actual, physical list of the friends you want to get together with. I've done this, and it helps to see the names written out, waiting to get a text from you. It may be exactly what they need in their own lives, a friend to talk to over a cup of coffee. I just pray no one ever finds that list of names, because taken out of context, it's just plain creepy.

I have a standing Friday night sushi date once a month with my friend Christian, and we both agree how nice it is to not decide where to eat each time. My friend Ashley and I get together every couple months to swap weird dating stories and cruise Target aisles on a Friday night, and that girl is good for my soul. When I first moved back to Springfield, my aunt and my cousins would come over to my house every Wednesday night, and we'd drink wine on the porch, chatting about everything under the sun moon. And like I mentioned earlier, I meet up with a girls' group every other Tuesday night, and I'm so, so thankful to have that diverse group of women in my life. If I was in a relationship right now, I don't think I'd have as much freedom to invest in all these friendships. The waiting is hard, but these consistent friendships make it sweeter.

And the last thing I'll throw out there if you're in a single season, is to invest in yourself. I've had years alone to get this adult acne thing figured out, and for that I am weirdly thankful. I don't have to shave my legs for anyone. How liberating! I can eat cereal for dinner three nights in a row and not feel guilty. I can talk to my dog in that weird dog person voice with no shame. I can watch a whole season of *Homeland,* and never have to change the channel (or my clothes). Someday another person might be sharing this house with me, but for now, I can live in it however I want. Independence is an empowering thing, so embrace it while you have it. Not that you can't when a partner is involved, but those moments of true independence are just harder to come by.

―――――

But I get it — all of this is easier typed on a screen than put into practice. Dating sucks. Swiping through duds is discouraging, especially when you get to the end and it literally says "there are no more men near you," because this has happened to me more times than I'd like to admit. Rejection hurts, and saying goodbye before you're ready is a pain I wouldn't wish on anyone. But I'm convinced it all is leading to that one that *will* work out. The only one that was meant to work out from the beginning. I'm learning to trust the process, learning to trust the One who can see the whole picture, when I can only see a couple pieces of it. God sees the ending to this story, and so I'm trusting Him with my middle. I'm slowly, and sometimes stubbornly, learning patience. I often go back to the promise He whispered to me on October 21, 2013, the day this whole mess started. I cling to it like a life raft sometimes, and it keeps me afloat:

You've served your time. I have better things for you.

When the loneliness kicks into high gear, I go back to this. There's a purpose in the waiting. There's healing in it. It's the pause button that we're forced to push — and it's a good thing. I'm preaching to the choir here, cause Lord knows I'm one to wallow in it on a Saturday night when everyone's Instagramming their adorable date nights, and I'm home organizing my closet. There's a calming peace about the waiting that I know I'll crave when I'm the one on the adorable date night, and so I write this reminder for myself, as much as for you. Use your waiting wisely. In the grand scheme of things, it's a blip. But it's your choice whether or not you make it a meaningful blip.

Use your waiting wisely. In the grand scheme of things, it's a blip. But it's your choice whether or not you make it a meaningful blip.

———

It was September 22, 2017, and I was liking another Facebook post of another friend flashing another engagement ring, and I was pretty much done. *When is it my turn?* I found myself asking God for an answer after seeing Grace, and Megan, and Lauren, and Jennifer, and so many other women whose marriages ended like mine, get their turns to finally see their heartbreak redeemed. It was bittersweet watching their prayers answered, to become the reality they had been waiting for. *When will I get my turn, Lord?*

As I was sulking, I felt a nudge to go sit in Poppy's room. She was at her dad's house, so her room was dark and still. Stuffed animals still lined up in a row playing school. A little box of hoarded treasures still spilled out on the floor. I curled up in her rocking chair with my great-grandmother's quilt that covers her bed, and I listened for the Lord ...

Maybe this season is not for you, but for Poppy. She is still so little. This one-on-one time you have with her is rare. She needs this time with you — just you — to recall when she's older. She needs to see your strength, your patience, your perseverance. She needs to remember this time with you, before I bring you into the next season. I promise you, it is coming. But this time is for her. Give her this season. Be here with her for this season. Just you. And just Poppy. It'll change later, the people, the dynamics, the environment, the struggles. But this season, with just the two of you, will never come around again. And I want her to be old enough to look back on it. Because she will need to pull from your strength one day.

I wiped tears on the quilt, accepting this season for what it is. No protest. I moved to her tiny crib-turned-toddler-bed, pulled the quilt up over my scrunched body, looked around at her world from this low, child-like vantage point, and I drifted off to sleep.

There are certain places where you can't not get real introspective. Pensive and thoughtful. About what's gone on before and what is coming up next. Squeezed into your kid's bed while she's away at her dad's. A quiet rooftop terrace in Italy. Alone on a beach, listening to the constant crashes of waves. I was on that beach just days after I was squeezed into that toddler bed, watching a young couple bob up and down out in the water just ahead of me, and I was reminded that my time is coming, too. But in that specific moment, just me and the empty chair next to me in the sand, I was right where I was supposed to be. For one of the first times I didn't feel jealousy or *why not me* — I felt happy for them. They waited for some length of time, too. And now they were here at this beach enjoying the fruits of their patience.

My time is coming, too. I'm just still in the waiting, the in-between. And I'm learning to be okay with that, because I have a tiny sidekick that needs me more than I need a helper.

This time is for her. Give her this season. Just you. And just Poppy.

CHAPTER EIGHT

THE PARENTING

Though the winter is long even richer, the harvest it brings;
though my waiting prolongs even greater, Your promise for me like a seed;
I believe that my season will come.

SEASONS BY HILLSONG WORSHIP

P arenting is hard, y'all. Single parenting is double hard. Because of … ya know … the math. But let me say one thing before I get too deep into this chapter — it is *all* hard. Whether you have a partner in this game or not, parenting is not an easy one to play. There are beautiful moments with your children that show you a glimpse of why God created you and how He loves us. There are blissful afternoons cuddling on the couch eating popcorn and watching *Moana* for the 1,000th time, and there's not a single place you'd rather be than right there, smelling that head of wild hair.

And then there are the low places. The rock bottoms. As Brené Brown puts it, the moments when you're face down on the arena floor. You're baffled as to why this demon child has taken up residence in your home, and don't you dare ask me for one more cup of goldfish. There are moments when you're both screaming and crying, and one of you is heaving with regret at the way you've just spoken to the other. (Hint: it's usually the grown up.) You teach them to control their feelings and not lash out in anger, but damn it, that tiny person pushes your buttons sometimes.

These are the moments that all parents feel, not just the single ones. And so I want to say here at the start of this parenting saga: we are *all* in it. We are all *deep* in it, together, friends. I am not a better mother because I've done it alone. I have simply lived a different season of motherhood than most. I am not more tired or more stressed or more *so done tonight at 8:00 with my glass of wine.* We are all learning the highs and lows of motherhood in our own ways, at our own pace, with our own stories, and with our own struggles. I will talk about my own experiences as a single mother — arena floor moments and all — but know this: mom shaming has no place anywhere near this book.

Now pour some wine of your own, because in this chapter you're gonna be mumbling a lot of *mmhmm girls* and a few *for the loves.*

A phrase I find myself repeating to Poppy all the time is, *I am just one person.* She's three right now, and even though three is obviously too young to understand the weird relationship that her parents have, I don't think it's too young to explain the difficulties on their own. *I am one person, and I can do one thing at a time,* I tell her. *At your Daddy's house, you have two grown ups to help you with things. Here at Mommy's house, you just have one. And so I need your help.*

I need help.

It's a phrase that moms don't say nearly enough, myself included. At my girls' group night recently, many of us were out with sick kids and out-of-town husbands, and so it was a smaller circle. It happened to be all the introverts who were there, so we were efficiently making our way through the evening. And a lot of us were struggling with some heavy stuff.

Michelle broke down talking about how her marriage had been rocky, and they couldn't seem to get in a good stride and actually stay there. She wanted a whole, strong family so badly, but things kept falling off the wagon. It was never quite there. She was overwhelmed with a toddler and a newborn and a new job and figuring out what her new normal would look like, and "I need help," she finally said through tears.

Jenn was eight months pregnant with her second, while her first was asleep upstairs, just barely a year old herself. She was anxious about how her life was about to get thrown into the newborn chaos in just a few short weeks, and she wanted to just keep him in her belly a bit longer, please? She felt her time with her oldest daughter would be missed, milestones would pass by without notice, as she started the whole movie over again from Scene 1, Baby 2.

Emma was struggling to balance the desire to start a family with her husband's uncertainty about having kids at all. Like ever.

Katrina struggled to reconcile the life she had left in New York City just a few months ago, with this new one she swore she'd never live — in flyover country, with a baby bump, driving a pickup truck.

Mallory was trying to figure out how to get back on the same page as her husband after a rough patch over the holidays.

Kate was exhausted by her wild toddler who refused to go to bed before 11:00 pm.

Females are strong as hell, so says the unbreakable Kimmy Schmidt. (Please watch that show immediately, it is side-splitting good.) And we can carry a heavy load on our shoulders for way longer than we should. So it was fitting that on that Tuesday night, we talked about chapter 8 in the book we're all reading together — *Rising Strong* by Brené Brown — which talked about asking for help. Learning that connection with another human happens when we learn to both give *and* receive help. It's vulnerable, and it's risky, and it's admitting that you can't do it all by yourself. But who doesn't love to feel needed? And who doesn't feel honored to be asked to weigh in?

And so when our village is struggling, we say, *How can we help? What can we do?* Because we are stronger together — *women* are stronger together. It's in our culture to be independent, buckle down and get 'er done. But we were designed for community. We were created to connect. We were wired to need help, but we just have to learn how to ask for it.

I asked Michelle how we could all help, and she jokingly replied, "Fix my marriage for me." I met her there, and replied, "Well, unfortunately, I'm not very good at marriage."

———

As a single parent, there's a piece of your parenting journey that you won't know is coming until you're knee deep in it. It's a piece that's rarely associated with parenting, and it's the same thread I've noticed being strung throughout so many aspects of my life, and even this book.

Grief. The absence of something that should be there. But isn't. Brené Brown, once again, describes grief perfectly as this: "We feel as if we're missing something that was invisible and unknown to us while we had it, but is now painfully gone."

Again, grief is not just reserved for death. Grieving the loss of a marriage, a relationship, a way of life you imagined for yourself that isn't coming to fruition. Grief often looks so different than we expect it to. And it affects far more parts of our lives than we realize.

Is this Debbie Downer really talking about grief again? Yes, she is.

Like holidays, for instance. For single parents, the season of cheer can actually be really bittersweet because of exactly what sister Brené said — *something invisible to us before is now painfully gone.* We imagined our holidays looking a certain way. We always pictured our Christmas mornings opening presents in our pajamas together; Daddy assembling toys and Mommy baking cinnamon rolls. But the reality is we spend half our Christmas mornings waiting anxiously for our kids to be dropped off. We're trading them back and forth between houses, loudly answering our dementia-riddled grandmother over and over, "She's at her dad's house, Grandma, I'm sorry." We're continually grieving those lost expectations in the back of our heads. Even in the times when that break from our kids is warmly welcomed, every parent still wants to be with their kids

> Grief often looks so different than we expect it to. And it affects far more parts of our lives than we realize.

on Christmas morning. That never goes away. It's taken a lot of getting used to, and four holiday seasons into being a single parent, I'm still trying to get my bearings sometimes.

But let's not just reserve our weird holiday moments for Christmas, let's spill it on over into every single parent's love-hate holiday: Mother's Day and Father's Day.

On Mother's Day, young single moms aren't usually greeted with breakfast in bed, a handmade card, and fresh picked flowers in a vase. Who's gonna get the baby out of the crib for all that? With kids too young to know what Mother's Day is, we wake up like any other day. We change diapers, prep bottles, wipe snot, and make our own damn breakfast. I said no mom shaming, but I've just come to live with the reality that Mother's Days for the first seven-ish years or so will probably just suck. No way around that. I figure a kid can't pull together a strategy or a surprise much earlier than that age, so I'm just really looking forward to Mother's Day 2021. Two years ago, I spent Mother's Day in urgent care with Poppy and her double ear infection. Last year, I spent it sick in bed myself while Poppy rummaged through the pantry eating God knows what. So technically they're getting better, right?

And hey single fathers, I know it might seem like a nice gesture to bring your ex-wife some balloons and a card on Mother's Day, signing it from your 2-year-old daughter that you share joint custody of, but it's just weird, okay? Don't do it. I understand the reasoning, and trying to show some ounce of *hey look, we're in this together.* But we're not *totally* in this together, remember? Especially when you extend the balloons to me with one arm, and your other arm is holding your new wife's hand. No bad feelings about that other hand, but it's all just weird. Too much weird. Don't add to the weird. When in doubt, no balloons.

But maybe worse than a Mother's Day where the mother still does all the work, is a Father's Day where the father is the one who left the mother. (Too soon?) I'll just put it out there in print — Father's Day for a single mother is straight up uncomfortable. I spent the first two Father's Days hanging out with my own dad, and avoiding Facebook at all costs. Married moms: dote on your husband all over the Internet that day; I'm seriously so glad he chose to go on this journey with you. This is not sarcasm—this is my genuine gratitude when dads choose to stay. My child's dad did not choose to stay, and so those doting posts are hard to read, and so single moms: just don't read 'em, okay? Stay away from Facebook, and do something nice for *yourself* that day.

On the first Father's Day after Poppy was born, a guy friend of mine sent me a message that said, "Happy Father's Day, Kelsey. Since you do the job of both, most of the time." That was probably the best Father's Day gift I have ever received, and I think of it every year on that day in June. Unfortunately that guy friend is happily married and has zero brothers. Ugh ... figures, right?

———

Recently, I was hanging out with some girlfriends who all happen to be married, and they were talking about the boundaries between their parents and their kids. Like when they find out their in-laws have taken their daughter to see Santa, unintentionally ruining the special trip they had marked on their calendar for just their little

1. Doctor's appointments. Do we need to wait for Dad? The nurses ask, and I cringe.

2. Father's Day. Just skip church and all Facebooking that day, okay? Trust me on this.

3. Showering. Like, what do you do with the kid?!

4. Holidays. Just, like, all of them. And maybe parties. And dinners. And get-togethers of all kinds.

5. Repair men who ask to speak to your husband. Nope, just me, buddy. That's why I called you.

6. When your OBGYN starts the "sex after pregnancy" talk at your 6-week postpartum appointment. I'm gonna stop you right there, Doc, and save both of us a few very awkward minutes.

7. When that same OBGYN asks what you're currently using for birth control at your annual exam four years later. Haven't had sex since the last time you asked, I remind him. Next question.

8. Anytime someone uses the term "hubby." I can't even. (I mean, I literally can't even, it seems.)

family of three. Or a grandmother who tells the granddaughter that she's taking her out for manis and pedis the week before school starts, and my friend's heart twisting a bit knowing she had planned the same special surprise date for just the two of them.

Conversations about husbands with friends who have actual husbands can be weird. There, I said it. You have stories to contribute, but they almost don't seem like *your* stories anymore. Because that person — that person who was happily married — seems so far removed from the You that's standing there in the conversation now. The ways you relate to their struggles can feel so different than the ways they intended them. You're not managing expectations with your parents and your kid — they're the ones you *want* to do those things with, because who else will you recall the memories with? The person you're managing expectations with is the child's other equally-involved parent. You're the one erasing school supply shopping dates from the calendar when your kid comes home from their dad's with a new backpack full of freshly sharpened pencils, crayons, scissors, and folders. Except it's harder to be upset than if it was a grandparent, because isn't it just as much his right to take her school supply shopping as it is yours?

Your stories, your anecdotes, seem harder to share in a group of married moms, because who can relate? Who can chime in with a *me, too?* Single parenting, and even just divorce alone, is incredibly isolating — and in weird ways that you never really picked up on until you're the one in the room unsure of your belonging. You always feel a a little bit like an outsider, no matter how inclusive your friends can be (and trust me, mine are the most inclusive bunch). The last thing you want is pity, but you also don't want people to think that it's just this inconvenient part of your life. It *is* your life. Reminders are waiting around every corner, and they don't really ever go away.

So if you have a friend who is a single parent, tell them they're doing a good job. And don't be surprised if they burst into tears when you say it, because our expectations are often being undercut, so we're caught off guard when they're exceeded. We don't have the built-in cheerleader, so we're easily startled when someone starts clapping on our behalf. If the ugly cry is triggered, just bear with us, okay?

Military moms, wives of traveling husbands, parents passing like ships in the night — none of it is easy. We can at least all say *me, too* to that one, can't we? Parenting is not for the faint of heart, no matter what parenting situation you find yourself in. So hear this, girlfriend: You're doing a good job. You have hard days and weeks and even months that seem to go on forever, but your kids are lucky to have you. God paired them up with you specifically, no one else. He knew you'd be the best mom for the job, so don't think for a second that you're screwing it all up. You're doing the best you can with what you have, and that is enough. You are enough.

———

Of course, like clockwork, having just returned from a night at her dad's house recently, Poppy didn't want to go to bed. Bedtimes on these "transition nights" are the hardest. I used to get frustrated when she'd drag it out for hours, but I finally noticed the pattern that it's always on her first night back with me. And so of course, then I felt like a terrible mom and finally cut her some slack.

So this night was one of those nights. As we laid in her bed together, I was running through the timeline for the next day (she's just like her mama, she likes to be prepared), and I noticed her eyes get big and her lip quiver just a tad when I told her Daddy was going to pick her up from school. She dipped her head low and said softly under her breath, "But I want Mommy to pick me up."

I tried to explain that sometimes it's Mommy and sometimes it's Daddy, but right now we need to go to bed. *For the love, we all need to go to bed.* But she's already up and out, walking around the room, avoiding sleep at all costs. So I go through all my usual tricks to get her back in bed, and she's just not having it. She's not angry, just sad and weepy. *Tired*, would be another word.

Finally I say it: "Does it make you sad that Daddy is picking you up tomorrow and not Mommy?"

She burst into tears. Bingo.

"It makes me sad cause I miss Cooper. And I miss Nana. And I miss Sydnee." She goes on naming off everyone in our family that she misses. And it just about melted my hardened its-8:30-I'm-tired-please-go-to-bed mama heart.

Then it occurs to me: at the ripe old age of three and a half, she is already experiencing loss. And in some ways, grief. And *that* is the thing that breaks my heart. Because I know it too well. Maybe

Maybe more painful than your own experiences with grief at the loss of your life expected is when you start to see your child picking up on the loss themselves.

more painful than your own experiences with grief at the loss of your life expected, is when you start to see your child picking up on the loss themselves.

We huddled together on her bed and talked about what we can do when we feel this sadness that comes with missing someone. We can think about past memories with them. We can think about the fun things we'll do together when we see them next. We talked about our family trip to the beach months earlier. We talked about seeing everyone at Christmas in just three weeks. We were just a couple of girls, lying in bed, talking through our grief.

"You love a lot of people don't you?" I asked as her eyes were finally getting heavy.

She nodded her head dramatically, lips still turned upside down.

"And a lot of people love you, too, you know that?"

She nodded again. I leaned in to kiss her cheek as she finally closed her eyes, and I whispered in her ear.

"And I was the very first one."

————

There are moments in single parenting when you think, *how the heck did I get here?* Standing at your front door discussing schedules with your ex-husband and his very pregnant wife. *You slept with her, and you slept with me, and now I can hardly have a conversation with you, and here's this kid we had together but not really together, and isn't all of this SO WEIRD to anyone else?*

Or standing in the parking lot of your kid's preschool on her first day, crying uncontrollable tears while your ex-husband's wife wraps her arms around you and hugs tightly. *I'm always praying for you,* she said. *I'm believing that God has great things for you,* she assured me. And all I could think was, *how the heck did I get here?*

Poppy started preschool in a whirlwind, and I wasn't at all ready for it. Dustin got a new job at a church, which happened to house one of the best preschools in town. With his job came a new work schedule, and we found ourselves suddenly needing to put Poppy in that preschool — and starting, ohhh, let's see … on Monday. Cool with that, Mom who's never put her kid in daycare ever? *Totally cool. I'm fine. Everything's fine!*

And so within a matter of days I'm wrapping my head around my kid starting preschool while also shuffling her into her classroom and praying she doesn't melt down. I should have been praying that *I* wouldn't melt down, because that's kind of what happened. Standing in your kid's classroom with your ex-husband and his wife, and reading the confusion on the teacher's face as she wonders who to call Mom. Seeing him put his hand on the small of her back in support of this sudden, new transition, and feeling overwhelmingly alone in my first-day-of-school-mom-jitters. Walking the halls of a church where Dustin is the one they know, and I am The Ex-Wife. It all can make a girl feel pretty insecure, and thus she becomes a crying mess in the parking lot with The New Wife. (Not to mention the awkward Will run-in at a coffee shop just a couple hours later. *Dear God, when will this day end?*)

This relationship, me and Melany The New Wife, has been an odd one. She's the girl I'm supposed to hate, but dang it, I like her. She's kind and gracious and good with Poppy, and I often wondered what she saw in Dustin in those early days. He had left his pregnant wife and was in the middle of a quarter life crisis when she entered the picture. Or maybe she had been in the background all along; I'll never really know for sure, but it doesn't matter. What I *do* know is that Melany has genuinely loved my child from the day she was born, and as weird as that sentence can seem when you think about this totally screwed up timeline of events, her presence in Poppy's life is something I am thankful for. As I mentioned before, and Poppy mentions *a lot,* she has a Mommy and a Daddy *and* a Melany. Doesn't everyone?

My relationship with Melany took on a whole new meaning when she became pregnant with her first — his second — child. If I had a hard time wrapping my head around Dustin getting remarried, his new wife getting pregnant was a whole new ballgame. On the one hand, it was salt in the wound. *I'll have a child with her, but not with you,* is what it felt like. But I also always knew that Dustin (or Melany for that matter) would never fully understand what it was like to go through a pregnancy and enter parenthood without a partner until they were both going through pregnancy and parenthood together.

My pregnancy was an unusual experience to say the least. And so by default, Dustin's experience with pregnancy was also pretty unusual. He visited his pregnant wife once a month for a couple hours to catch up, and then returned to his bachelorhood. He had never actually been through a pregnancy with a woman, despite the fact that he had a three-year-old daughter. When he spilled the beans to me that Melany was pregnant, he looked absolutely terrified. Because he knew as well as I did that he had never actually done this before. And so when I got the news that he would be present for a full nine months of pregnancy, even if it was with another woman, part of me kicked my feet up with my bowl of buttered popcorn and thought, *well he's in for a surprise.*

I could tell those nine months wore on him — he looked more and more tired with every Poppy handoff. But I also saw another change in him during that time — he grew up. For lack of a better word, he got his shit together. He became more consistent and reliable — two words I never would have used to describe him when we were together. In some ways, I feel like I got his worst years, and she's getting his best. Like she's reaping the rewards of my hard work. I'm sure they have their own struggles, like any couple, but he's choosing to stay married to her, and that's a choice he wasn't man enough to make with me.

One afternoon, Dustin and I were standing in the parking lot of Poppy's preschool while I was picking her up, and we were making our usual small talk. I asked about Melany, (she was eight months pregnant at that point), and he was honest.

"She's nervous," he said. "She sees how hard you've worked with Poppy, teaching her to be kind and patient, and she compares herself to you. She wonders if she'll be able to be as good of a mom as you've been to Poppy."

I'm glad I was wearing sunglasses that day, because the tears that swelled up in my eyes in that moment would not have gone unnoticed. *Hold the phone, she compares herself to me?!* I couldn't fathom it, and I still can't sometimes. My part in our weird divided family is so ingrained in my head that it's hard for me to put myself in another character's shoes — especially hers. But if I really admit it, I compare myself to her all the time. *Why did he choose her and not me? What did she have that I didn't? What did I have that she didn't, that he didn't want?* And so maybe it's not that far-fetched for one mom to compare herself to another. Especially two moms with the same baby daddy. *Gosh, my life is weird.*

Over the entire nine months, there was one person who never let me forget that my ex-husband and his new wife were having a baby, and that person was the adorably innocent Penelope Rose.

"Hey Mommy, do you know what?" she'd say.

"What?" *I knew what.*

"I'm gonna have a baby sister."

I'd act surprised, and we'd talk about Baby Sister and how she'd cry, and I'd secretly pray that she'd cry more than a normal baby (because ex-wives have a hard time not being cynical). We'd have this conversation about 237 times per day, and that poor little thing had no idea the salt she was pouring in my wound. I can laugh at the irony of all this now, but on the days when this mama was tired of the general Mom gig, and she'd bring up that beloved Baby Sister, I would have to bite my tongue. Hard.

"Ya know what Sweet P, I know you're excited about your baby sister, but let's talk about something else, okay?" *Or Mommy might lose it.*

And then enter single parent aha-moment of the day — my kid will have an entirely separate life that I'll know nothing about. She has a room and a bed and toys and even a sibling that I'll never know. It's a weird phenomenon, but one that I was actually pretty accustomed to. My parents had divorced when I was in kindergarten, so I was very familiar with the two houses, two routines, two families. I take solace in the fact that my parents' divorce didn't affect me much because I was too young to remember much about life before they split. Like Poppy, it was all I ever knew. I remember a handful of moments before they divorced — hello, snakes and spaghetti dinners — but that's it. My prayer is that Poppy will grow up like I did. Rolling with the two families thing, because she doesn't really know any different.

But the one thing I never even considered when I was a kid was the impact that two families must have had on my parents, trying to raise three kids in two different houses. Each of my parents saw their own side of my life, but I was the only one living in both lives. And so trust comes into play — trusting that the other parent is providing a quality life when they're on duty. Even trust that you, the child, aren't choosing a favorite.

I'm finally proud of who I am. I understand now that I'm not a mess, but a deeply feeling person in a messy world. When someone asks me why I cry so often, I say, "For the same reason I laugh so often — because I'm paying attention."

GLENNON DOYLE

I'm on the other side of this messed up equation now, and the perspective is nothing short of eye-opening. Poppy has two places she lives her life, and I am just one of them.

———

I picked up Poppy one evening, and Melany answered the door with a 39-week baby bump poured into a beautiful flowing floral maxi dress. She looked tired. Uncomfortable. Like the kind of

It's New Year's Eve. We spun and danced and laughed and let loose in the kitchen, music turned up as high as it could go. It was well past her bedtime, and it was well worth it. The joy on her face was unmatched, and I wished I could freeze that moment for just a bit longer. I also wished I could enjoy it with someone. Recall it later with them and laugh some more. But something in me kept at it again — she needs to remember just you. She needs just you right now. *I know this season of waiting and wondering will pass, but it is a constant struggle.*

So here I am in bed, 30 minutes before midnight, and recalling it. Her pure unfiltered joy, dancing in the kitchen with her mother on New Year's Eve. And I am so thankful to get to be her dance partner. She makes the load I carry — the isolation, loneliness, grief, and longing — she makes it all a bit lighter. If I didn't have her, this journey would be so different, more bumpy. She grounds me. Brings me back to center. She's my little pigtailed compass. She comes with a whole set of struggles all her own, but I'll take those any day over walking this winding road alone. I love you Poppy Rose. Happy New Year.

uncomfortable any 39-week pregnant lady feels. And the kind of uncomfortable that any woman feels, standing at her front door greeting her husband's ex-wife. *I feel it, too, girlfriend.* We made our small talk, exchanged clean clothes, gathered backpacks and lunch boxes and stuffed animals passed between houses. Dustin came to the door, and I asked about their plan for when the baby comes. *What about Poppy? If she's with you, do you want me to take her back? If she's with me, do you want her there to meet the baby? Did you ever think we would be having this conversation? Like when I was also 39 weeks pregnant, but hadn't heard from you in over a month?* Those last two questions I kept to myself.

Mid-conversation, Melany rubbed her belly with a slight cringe and walked away. I'm guessing to puke or to pee or just to escape the awkward. Or all three. Dustin continued to talk about their plans for the birth, the birthing classes, the doula, the family members that would be there, oversharing as usual. I couldn't help but think of the weeks leading up to Poppy's birth. I was surrounded by support from my own family and friends. I had my own list of people I wanted there, I had my own bag packed. I was preparing for her birth in the same way every other mother does — or at least tries to, because how can you actually prepare to push a human out of your body?

But I was also preparing myself for moments that few other mothers prepare for. *When do I let my estranged husband in the room? Do I take a picture of that moment, or do I leave that up to him? I certainly don't want a picture of that, but will Poppy wonder where that picture is when she's older? Will he visit her in the hospital after the delivery? Will his family visit? Will he want to stay the night in my hospital room with her? Oh God, please don't let him stay the night in that room. Will he protest when I write my last name on her birth certificate? Will the nurses ask why my mom is in the room and he is not?*

In the midst of the rolodex of memories cycling through my mind, he said something that both infuriated me and made me laugh at how little he really understood about his first daughter's birth.

"I know I was only in the hallway, and not in the room," he said, "but from what I heard, it was pretty intense."

Yes. Yes, he said this. He said this to the woman who pushed his child out of her body without a drop of pain medication in her system. He said this to the woman who took the nurse's advice when she suggested that screaming helps release the pain. *Oh, you want me to scream, Nurse? Gladly.* I screamed with every push, not just because the pain was unimaginable after three straight hours of pushing, but because I wanted one particular person standing on the other side of that door to hear it. To hear every shred of agony, every ounce of grief. To hear each scream as a message straight to his ears. *Yeah, I'm in here. And you're out there. And why did you make it this way?*

Yes, Dustin. It was pretty intense. It was more intense than I expected, too. An intensity I will never forget. Intense pain. Intense pressure. Intense grit that I didn't know I had. Intense trust that she would come when she was ready, and that my body would know what to do. And then suddenly, as if she had reached her limit, too — intense release. Intense pouring out of strength, from my body to hers, as she slipped sweetly into this world and took her first breath. Intense relief. Intense love. But still, a twinge of intense sadness that would continue to linger years later — even typing this now — that this moment looked so different than how I had always imagined it.

Something — someone — was missing. And despite the unspeakable joy that Penelope Rose brought me, making me a mom that day, I was keenly aware that you were out there, and I was in here, and that wasn't how it was supposed to be.

Intense doesn't scratch the surface.

It was a couple weeks later when Melany went into labor, and in some weird way, I envied her. She made a baby with him, and he *didn't* leave her. She was pregnant for nine months, and he was there *with* her. She scream-pushed that baby out, and he was there holding her hand. I envied her in the same way I envied any woman who got to go through that experience with a partner.

I held Poppy a little tighter that night before bed, remembering my own labor and delivery, and when I held her skin-to-skin on my chest just minutes after she was born. Tonight, she instinctively nuzzled in for a bit, and then like clockwork, pulled away and said, "I'm not a baby, Mom!"

"Yeah, I know, but you're *my* baby."

———

Poppy told me about 3,591 times today that she missed her dad. The first few hundred times were sweet, and I could smile through them. The last few hundred times made me want to throw my coffee across the room. The second to the last time made me feel like a terrible mom, and the very last time made us both switch over to Ugly Cry Face.

The second to last time she said it, I was giving her a bath. I honestly cannot remember the last time I gave her a bath. I know,

Mom of the Year. But it's winter, and my house is cold, and I'm just crossing my fingers that her dad is doing it when she's over there. I'm wondering now if he's been hoping I'm doing it when she's over here, which leaves us both with a kid who terribly needs a bath. *Sorry, kid.*

I've also been avoiding baths because she hates them. Occasionally, I'll get lucky and catch her on a rogue night where she frolics and swims and makes soap bubble beards, and I'll shoot up a little *thank you* prayer for an easy one, finally. But most nights go about like this night did: she starts out excited to jump in the tub, and then realizes the actual bathing part will require the top half of her body to be wet, and she's immediately done with the whole charade. So it went tonight, and this exhausted mama was fresh out of energy to coax her through the suddenly traumatizing bath routine. And so it was no surprise that when she blurted it out again — *I miss Daddy* — as I poured a cup of water over her head, it was the straw that broke the Mama's back. I, too, was immediately done with the whole charade. Already feeling like a pretty terrible mother for the day, I threw the cup in the tub, and made some sarcastic remark about also missing her Daddy but in a very different way and for very different reasons, and of course instantly regretting my childish outburst.

She watches your every move, Kels, I reminded myself as I sobbed into my hands, sitting on the toilet next to the tub. *She hears every word, that little sponge.* I pulled myself together, and quickly rinsed her half washed body and hair, both of us now in tears. I wrapped her in a towel, and scooped her up so we could calm down together in her rocking chair. We sat rocking in silence for a good ten minutes, as I prayed my usual: *I can't do this, God. I can't do this alone forever. I could hardly do it today. I need your help.*

As I rocked her, I struggled with what to say to her. On the one hand, I want her to understand that it's painful for me to hear that she misses her dad so much. On the other hand, I know, because he's told me, that she says the same thing about me when she's at his house. On yet another hand, I don't want her to ever feel guilty for missing him. I don't want her to think it's bad or ever be afraid to tell me so. And so I'm left hanging out with this three-handed monster that I guess I have to just keep to myself? Swallowing my pride and forcing an "it's okay" every time she says she wants him over me? And harbor that bitterness where? Where is there space in that hole he left in my heart to add even more grief, pile on more anger, throw in another grudge?

> One day we will look back on days like this and realize that the little things mattered a lot more than we ever thought they would.
>
> MORGAN HARPER NICHOLS

This is the ugly side of single parenting. The side that doesn't get talked about, the side that looks a lot like complaining. As much as it feels like complaining, it's also just our reality. These inner battles of what to tell your kid, what to keep to yourself, what needs explaining, and what needs shielding. It's a never-ending battle with new struggles popping up on the regular. I haven't figured out how to handle all these yet, but one thing I come back to often: we are *both* her parents. We love her equally, and she loves us equally. That is fact, not opinion. Another fact: I will not be the parent

It breaks my heart that she won't ever get to experience her parents under the same roof. It breaks my heart that she only gets one at a time.

It breaks my heart that she's already feeling the weight of that on her tiny shoulders — shoulders that shouldn't be carrying anything of the sort.

who badmouths the other, as much as I want to throw him under the bus sometimes. It's a hard choice that I have to make every single day of this journey, and one I know I will make for the rest of her life.

We sit rocking back and forth, back and forth, until she looks up at me and sweetly says "I'm sorry, Mommy."

I held her tiny face in my hands, and made my choice. "You didn't do anything wrong; you do *not* need to say you're sorry. It's okay to miss your Daddy. It's okay."

Her little bottom lip is turned out and quivering, and just the sight of it makes mine do the same. She is so tender-hearted, she feels everything for everyone around her. It breaks my heart that she won't ever get to experience her parents under the same roof. It breaks my heart that she only gets one at a time. It breaks my heart that she's already feeling the weight of that on her tiny shoulders — shoulders that shouldn't be carrying anything of the sort.

She lays her head back down on my chest, my shirt drenched from her wet hair. I squeeze my eyes shut as hard as I can, trying to snap myself back to reality. And she squeezes in one more:

"I just really miss my Daddy."

———

A fresh sage, thyme, and lemon zest candle. Some melaleuca oil rubbed on my face in the problem areas, followed by a little coconut oil and lavender, cause adult acne, can I get an amen? Maybe this is too many smells and aromas. Too many things overtaking my senses? Maybe I was trying to cover something up? Could it be the giant is-this-ADHD meltdown Poppy had that evening? The one that went on for nearly an hour? The one with all the screaming, kicking, throwing toys, slamming doors, and hitting herself. The one that made me lock myself in the bathroom just so I could cry out loud, hoping she heard me. Because sometimes it makes her stop screaming if she sees me crying, but also because I'm actually crying. Like heaving, eyes squeezed shut, audible noises coming out, crying.

When I came out of the bathroom, and her screaming finally turned to crying, and she actually wanted me to hold her, we both sat on the floor in the kitchen and cried some more. I tried to explain in the simplest three-year-old terms why we do not act like that, young lady. The whole time knowing its going in one ear and out the other, and also she's three. Well, she will be in exactly four days. *Wow. Three? Are you sure God? Are you sure it's been that long? Errr ... ONLY that long? Are you sure about any of this that you're doing?*

After we finished our cry sesh, we brushed our teeth, picked up all the strewn toys, and went to bed. I allowed one book instead of my plan to ban all books for the rest of her life, because maybe I'm not a terrible mom, though I feel like a terrible mom tonight, and maybe one book will help her like me again? The things we tell ourselves. We read our one book, I skipped a few pages unde-tected because mama's tired of momming for the day, and ready for some fresh sage, thyme, lemon zest, lavender, coconut, melaleuca mom time. We finished our skimmed book, and I knelt down to pray to Jesus, as we say each night. I'm so done, but I feel that tug that says, *don't skip this part, she needs to see it, and you need to say it.* I prayed in a way that I could only hope a three-year-old understands, and her tired mama could muster:

> *Dear Jesus. We're sorry for the screaming and the kicking and the throwing. Forgive us for all the ugliness we had tonight. Help us to stay calm and ask for help when our feelings get so big. Help us to always speak to each other with kindness and love. Help us to just pray when we forget all these things. And if you would have it, please send us a helper. Amen.*

———

From the time Poppy was born, she's been traveling. I made the eight hour drive to Nashville when she was just eight weeks old, and I've made that drive probably 15 times since then, almost always just me and my little bird as my co-pilot. I used to brag about how great of a traveler she was. She could adapt to anything, sleep anywhere. Trips with her were relatively easy.

But around the time Poppy turned three, her reaction to change began to shift. The traveling was suddenly a nightmare. In fact, anything that broke her routine made her turn into a tiny, curly-haired monster. She started having these meltdowns, and even as I would try to describe the magnitude of them to other moms, and they would nod in agreement, I felt deep down that these were different.

They were intense. There was a lot of screaming. Like, *a lot*. Nothing I said would get through to her, and it was like she had this tunnel vision of rage that nothing could break except for her own exhaustion. They weren't the usual 10-15 minute tantrums that just needed a distraction; these were full on battles that lasted an hour or more. They were painful and draining, and I'm 99% sure my neighbors probably thought I was a terrible mother.

I felt like no one believed me when I said these meltdowns were different. I didn't have a spouse to witness it and say, *yes there's something off here,* and *no you are not crazy, dear.* Dustin said she rarely melted down for him, and when she did they were mild and easily recovered. *Awesome. So it's just me.*

A few weeks later, I read this Instagram post by interior designer Emily Henderson, and may have audibly shouted, "YES! THIS!" She described a meltdown her son had that evening, and it sounded all too familiar. Over the top, uncontrollable screaming, all starting with a very, very small trigger. She said it best in these lines:

> *I need to know more about what triggers these "meltdowns." I put that in quotes because it sounds adorable and slow, and not like the violent fits that we have experienced. ... Who has witnessed their child "meltdown" to the point where you wanted to video it to show a professional? Have you ever asked yourself "is this normal?"*

I could have written that caption, myself. Funny how even just a quick photo and a caption by a complete stranger on the Internet can make you feel a little less alone. *She gets it. She sees it, too.*

Finally, on a trip to Nashville, I got my witness. We were at my mom's house, having some downtime, and something in the playroom set her off. She went into full meltdown mode (not the slow, adorable kind), and I tried desperately to calm her down. At first, I didn't want my mom to see her so upset, and I felt embarrassed that I couldn't get control of my own child. And then, like every other time, I just gave up. I sat sobbing on the couch downstairs, while my mom tagged in and tried to calm Poppy upstairs. Tears streamed down my face uncontrollably as my dear mother's stern voice tried to reason with the hysterical kid. I hadn't heard that voice since my own childhood. Poppy's screams were getting more scratchy, and I could tell her voice was going out. That's how hard she screams, for the record.

Eventually, her screams turned to cries, her rage turned to exhaustion, and she came down off her high. A few minutes later, my mom carried her downstairs, and the words out of her mouth were such a relief:

"That was not normal."

Finally. Finally someone was in my corner. Finally someone else could see this start to finish, and agree that it was over the top. Finally I could figure this thing out.

My mom rocked Poppy in the rocking chair, as we started talking through options. ADD, ADHD, hypersensitivity, anger management issues, extreme tantrums, we googled all the things that afternoon. And just like my running pregnancy joke, I was not the first person to google any of it. It was one of the rare times when I felt like I had a partner to help me troubleshoot a parenting issue. (I mean, other than Emily Henderson.) Every parenting choice, discipline decision, routine idea — I make all of those calls by myself. And I didn't realize how exhausted I was from that pressure, until I found myself in a dilemma where I was totally lost. I needed help, but I didn't really know how or who to ask for it.

After a long afternoon that left all three of us drained of all energy, we finally concluded one thing that changed the course of my parenting from that day forward: I needed to read the book *The Highly Sensitive Child* by Elaine N. Aron.

Several years ago, my brother Grant and his wife Sheila began to notice patterns in one of their daughters' behavior that seemed similar to what I was experiencing with Poppy — over-the-top reactions to really small problems — and a friend of theirs recommended they read this book. They both read it cover to cover, and bought my mom a copy to read as well, since she was a frequent caregiver. It totally changed how they approached their parenting, and so I grabbed my mom's copy off the bookshelf that day and started reading. I was desperate for information to help me understand why Poppy was acting this way, and how I could help her.

I laid on my mom's bed that afternoon, skipped dinner with my brother's family that evening, and read chapter after chapter of that wonderfully eye-opening book. A moment in the first few pages made me burst into tears, and I knew I was on the right track: "No wonder you worry that you may be doing something wrong. You have no one to help you. ... You're struggling with issues that the [other parenting] books don't talk about ... "

I laughed out loud at that starting line, and then immediately felt the frog in my throat. This described how I often felt reading parenting advice on blogs at 3:00 in the morning when my newborn was wide awake. *Tag team it with your husband,* they would say. *You need a break, and he can take his turn,* they would suggest. I imagined the writers happily typing this out, and marveling at what great advice they were giving their readers. *Deep breaths, Kelsey.* It was around that point in the articles that I would say some special words, throw my phone across the bed, and just pray. *Please, Lord, put her to sleep. I can't do this alone; please just let her sleep.*

I borrowed the book about highly-sensitive children from my mom, and that pesky frog stayed there in my throat through most of the chapters. I finally had a resource that could accurately describe my child and give me real advice on how to help her. I finished that book with the realization that *my* reaction to my child's emotions is as important, if not more important, than my child's reactions to her own emotions. I came home from that Nashville trip, and was weirdly excited for Poppy's next meltdown so I could test out my new strategies. Like clockwork, I got my chance that night, and I'll never forget it. She started into her screaming and kicking and throwing things. And I did something I had never done before — I sat calmly on her bed and waited. I didn't raise my voice at her, I didn't cry, I hardly even talked to her at all. I kept my own emotions in check, and just kept reminding her that I was there for her, and ready to talk when she was.

It didn't take long for Poppy to notice the difference in my reaction, and she was hilariously confused. *Holy crap, this is working.* I sat quietly twiddling my thumbs, and she calmed herself down within about 15 minutes. Then she fell into my waiting arms, and we both cried and cried. Hers were tears of exhaustion, and mine were tears of relief. I felt like I had just solved one of those never-ending 10,000 piece puzzles — the ones you see across the room, halfway completed, and think for sure you can be the one to solve it. But a few minutes in, you realize why it's been sitting here unfinished for days, and you give up like all the others before you. I had solved this impossibly adorable puzzle. Cracked her code. I had figured out my child, and there's no better feeling than that.

In the months that followed, her meltdowns were shorter and fewer. And after each one, we would sit down together and talk about our big emotions. We both learned together how to tame our reactions, and channel our frustrations. We came up with a saying to help calm us down when we felt the heat rising:

Small problem, small reaction. I'd hold my palms a few inches apart from each other, like I was holding a tiny box with my hands.

Big problem, big reaction. Then I'd spread my hands wide, like I was holding a box of diapers to help her understand the difference.

And it's pretty adorable to hear a three-year-old try to pronounce the word *reaction*.

Sometimes she gets it in those critical moments before a meltdown, and she can step back from the ledge on her own. Sometimes she doesn't, and slams the door in my face while I wait quietly outside her room. Sometimes I get it, and brush off little things that easily frustrate me. Sometimes I don't, and I'm the one doing the door slamming, and realizing my big reaction is because of a very small problem.

We're both learning. We're still figuring each other out. We're both learning how to manage our emotions, and hold each other accountable. Sometimes she sees that I'm getting upset about something and sings me that annoying Daniel Tiger song, "When you're feeling frustrated, take a step back, and ask for help." Those are humbling moments, when my three-year-old gives me a dose of my own medicine.

I've found that longer transitions between activities, keeping our routines consistent, and over-communicating our feelings and events of the day has helped her tremendously. She's just like her mother, I suppose — she likes to know what's coming next. (Remind me never to throw her a surprise party.)

As badly as I want to blame these struggles on Dustin's decision to leave, and my lack of a helper, not all of my challenges with Poppy are because her parents are divorced. Some are just regular kid stuff. Some are just highly-sensitive kid stuff. Some stuff she'll grow out of, and some stuff will just be part of her personality. We've got many more years ahead of us to screw up and pair big reactions to small problems. Lord help us.

Even now as I type this, the glow of my laptop screen is illuminating my dark room and the little face asleep on the pillow next to mine. I used to put my foot down when she'd push back at bedtime, begging to sleep in my bed. *I don't want her to get in the habit,* I used to think, in my mom voice. And then she figured out how to get me to say *yes* every single time — ask me at 2:30 am. She started waking me up — and totally freaking me out — quietly standing next to my bed in the middle of the night, asking to climb in. She quickly figured out that I am 99% more likely to let her climb on in than to leave my cozy covers and walk her back her room. *Smart girl.*

After a couple weeks of this, I noticed we both were sleeping better when we were sleeping together. The nights that she's at her dad's house, I miss her round little face drooling all over my sheets. I miss her throwing her pillow on the floor and pulling mine closer so we could share. I even miss her flopping and kicking and sleeping exactly like her dad did — constantly moving. I was trying to make a lesson out of sleeping in her own bed, but it usually just led to a meltdown, and somebody was in tears. I was giving her a big reaction to a small problem — she just wanted to be close to me. So I'm learning to savor this season when she begs to share my covers, because I know it won't last forever.

I can't shake the moment lying in her bed a few months ago, praying for God to change my circumstances, and He so graciously reminded me to keep sitting in the one I'm given.

This time is for her. Give her this season. Just you. And just Poppy.

She needs me all to herself, and that makes the big problems turn back into small problems. And who the heck else is sleeping in this bed with me? *Climb in, kid.*

CHAPTER NINE

THE STORY

With skinned knees and bruised hearts, we choose owning our
stories of struggle over hiding, over hustling, over pretending.
When we deny our stories, they define us. When we run from struggle,
we are never free. So we turn toward the truth and look it in the eye.

BRENÉ BROWN

I'll cut to the chase: sharing your story with a bunch of strangers can be downright scary. Especially strangers on the Internet — ya know, that cold, dark place where people hide behind usernames and forget that real humans are on the other sides of their screens. It's pulling back your sleeves to show your scars, gnarly as they may be. It could even be wounds that haven't yet turned to scars, they're still open wide and prone to more pain. It's a vulnerable state, but it's one I am believing more and more is worthwhile.

It can be especially tricky for introverts to tell their stories. In high school, I was voted "Most Quiet," and I was super pissed about it. It drove me nuts when peers would throw out questions like, "Why are you so quiet?" or "Why don't you talk more?" So, I'll step onto my soapbox real quick here and shoot right back, *how would you like me to answer those questions? Were you looking for a specific reason for my shyness? Were you hoping it was some medical issue with my vocal chords, so you can feel less awkward about the whole conversation?* So, Most Quiet was not my favorite label. I'm still bitter; don't mind me.

In fact, I much prefer a phrase that a woman emailed me recently: *the silent power beneath it all.* Ah, yes. That's much better. We are not shy or quiet or timid or afraid — we are the silent power beneath it all. We are reaching inward to make decisions and process conflict and see who we can trust with our stories. And so when an *inward* thinker shares her raw, in-between story *outwardly*, it can be the power beneath it all. It can be the story that another woman needs to hear to get through her middle, too. That's the woman who needs to hear a "me, too," even if it's not the loudest voice in the room.

I shared my story for the first time on May 12, 2015. It was a blog post that I wrote — my very first blog post ever, in fact — and I didn't think anyone would read it. My business was barely gaining traction, no one knew my name, much less that I had been through a divorce in the two years prior. I'd had an inkling to write for quite some time, but I didn't exactly know what I needed to write about.

Then one day I found myself standing in my backyard looking up at the sky with tears streaming down my face, listening to my screaming baby inside. And it hit me: *write. Write now. Right now. Write all of this down.*

So I went inside — tended to the screaming baby first, of course — and then sat on my bed and opened up my laptop. I didn't think, I didn't outline, I didn't try to come up with a clever intro or a catchy title, I just started typing what I was feeling and what I was thinking, and how I ended up crying in my backyard. I wrote about my marriage, my divorce, my pregnancy, Poppy's first weeks home. I wrote several thousand words before I felt settled, before my mind cleared up, and I could think straight again. I sat back and realized I had my first blog post. And it had nothing to do with business or entrepreneurship or design or anything that my work was centered around at the time.

> If something inside you is real, we will probably find it interesting, and it will probably be universal.
>
> ANNE LAMOTT

And then I knew what I needed to be writing about.

Before I could change my mind, I got out my phone, opened Instagram, and wrote a post announcing that I was starting a blog, and it would launch on This Arbitrary Date. I hit Post. Done. It was out there. I knew my people-pleasing personality meant that I couldn't turn back now - now that I had shared it with all of *maybe* 100 followers who probably didn't even see that late night spontaneous post. But I'm an obliger, as I heard someone call it recently, and so I must oblige the strangers on the Internet.

This Arbitrary Date came a few weeks later — May 12, 2015 — and my heart was pounding out of my chest as my mouse hovered over the Publish button. This was it, there was no turning back. I promised them the post, they were commenting about wanting to read the post, and here I was publishing the post. One minute I was just some freelance designer who really liked Squarespace, and the next I was the single mom entrepreneur with a crazy story.

I had no idea what would come of that post, but the day I published it, I got absolutely nothing done on my to do list. Instead, I was reading the hundreds of comments that were pouring in. People from all over the world were reading my dirty laundry, and — what's this? They're actually feeling inspired?! Encouraged?! They're saying, *me, too,* and *I've been there,* and even *thank you?!*

I was blown away. Floored. Again: sharing your story with the unpredictable strangers on the Internet can be downright scary. You're allowing yourself to be vulnerable with no guarantee of how people will react, and how it will change their opinions about you. But — it can also be downright inspiring. I got emails from other women who were in the midst of divorce and didn't feel quite so alone after reading my story. I read comment after comment from moms of all kinds who were sharing their own struggles and cheering me on in mine. To this day, people stumble upon my blog through that post, and leave a comment about how it impacted their day — it's one of the most viewed posts in my archive, and it's definitely the one I'm most proud of. It was the day I realized my story was way more influential than I realized. It was brave and impassioned, and I found myself as the silent power beneath it all.

As I've written down story after story for this book and dug out old journals from my basement, I've noticed something. The result of writing this book has been a linear documentation of my story, from point A to point B. Which may seem obvious, because hello, it's a book, but as the writer of the book and the owner of the story, it feels big. Stepping back and seeing the entire rollercoaster as a whole, it's easy to spot the patterns. One of those patterns, and the one I didn't even realize was a pattern until writing this book, is just that — *writing*. When my life felt too heavy to carry, I grabbed whatever blank paper or cursor on a screen I could find and started writing. It was my unconscious therapy that I didn't even notice I was practicing.

In the days after Dustin left, I had that urge to write down my anger in that old day planner. On my first night in the hospital with Poppy, I was exhausted beyond belief, but forced myself to pull out the notebook in my bag and write down her birth story before the baby brain washed it all away. In the months I dated Will, I wrote and I wrote and I wrote some more. Now, on the particularly hard days with my favorite strong-willed little girl, I put her to bed and head straight for my laptop to dump out my frustrations. So it's no surprise that on that evening in my backyard, when I was tired and defeated, my natural instinct was to write.

> For every kind of soul you meet with a beautiful story to tell, may you know that you are worthy of being seen that way as well.
>
> MORGAN HARPER NICHOLS

The more I write down my story, the more it's no longer something I shy away from or feel ashamed to admit. It's become something I've staked a claim in. A piece of me that shaped my entire perspective on life and love and just plain being alive. Like the quote at the beginning of this chapter: *I turned toward the truth and looked it in the eye.* It is a hard story and a winding story and an ugly beautiful mess that I get to call my own.

In the same way, your story is just that — it's *yours*. It's yours to share or yours to hold close. It's your choice how, when, and if

> Breathe deep and breathe loud. The person on the mat next to you might be holding in theirs and need the reminder.

you share your story at all. There is no wrong answer here, there's only *your* answer. But my reason for sharing can be summed up nicely in something the instructor said one morning at my hot yoga class: "Breathe deep and breathe loud. The person on the mat next to you might be holding in theirs and need the reminder."

———

I sat at a quiet coffee shop in Rome, Italy, across from my brother Taylor, who was doodling in his notebook and overanalyzing his espresso, and I finished a book. No, not this one you're reading, that would come a few months later. I finished reading Anne Lamott's *Bird by Bird,* by Anne Lamott. I was in the very beginning stages of writing this book (the one you're holding), of sharing my story in a bigger, more permanent way than I ever had. It's in those first stages, the start of something big, that the doubts most easily sneak in. They want you to quit before you even begin. They don't think you can do it. I was feeling that already. *This story is too big, a book is too public, there are too many hearts at stake. I'm not cut out for this.*

But on one of the very last pages of her book, Anne's words jumped off the page at me, snapping me back to reality:

> *... to have written your version is an honorable thing to have done. Against all odds, you have put it down on paper, so that it*

won't be lost. And who knows? Maybe what you've written will
help others, will be a small part of the solution. You don't even
have to know how or in what way, but if you are writing the
clearest, truest words you can find and doing the best you can to
understand and communicate, this will shine on paper like its
own little lighthouse. Lighthouses don't go running all over an
island looking for boats to save, they just stand there shining.

Honorable, against all odds. Stand there shining. See, sharing your
story doesn't have to be complicated. It's simple really — *the clearest,*
truest words you can find. All anyone really wants is for our stories
— ourselves — to be respected, accepted, and known. We want to
know that our stories are not only heard, but they are honored and
validated to be true.

A few weeks after Poppy's half-sister was born, I found myself
talking with Dustin at our drop-off. I asked how the baby was doing,
and he answered honestly: *newborns are really, really hard.* I chuckled
in agreement, but he validated my story further.

"I had no idea what I was putting you through, and I'm sorry for
that," he acknowledged.

It was the clearest, truest words I had been waiting years for
him to not just say, but to experience. I always knew he wouldn't
truly *get it* until he had a child with his new wife, in his new life. He
wouldn't understand what it was like to care for a newborn 24/7
alone, until he had to care for a newborn 24/7 period.

And so as we stood in the doorway talking about his second
child, I finally felt like his first was validated. That season was seen
by him. *This* season — and it's heaps of loneliness, exhaustion, and

grief as a single mother — was seen by him. He was beginning to understand my story — to accept it, respect it, and know it to be true.

Your story might look really different than mine. If I can boil this way, way down, there are two groups of women I wrote this book for. The first is the woman with the fairytale story. She got the husband, then she had the kids, and they're all living happily ever after behind a white picket fence. This is not sarcastic, but I just mean that you've checked the right boxes in the right order. Or at least what society tells us is right. This might be a small group.

The second group of women is the bigger group, and I'd be willing to bet that most of you are in this group. This is the woman whose story looks different than what she expected. This is the woman who woke up to a reality that she did not dream about as a child. She's enduring grief and trauma and pain and a remodeling of her life that she wasn't ready for.

She's the single girl in her 30s who thought she'd have so many more boxes checked by now.

She's the mother who just adopted her first child, and is struggling to reconcile her joy in finally being a mother and her guilt for tearing this child away from everything she's ever known.

She's a 20-something who's faced miscarriage after miscarriage, and has found herself now fostering and adopting teenage girls not much younger than she is.

She's a seasoned mother of five who has taken in and fallen in love with dozens of foster children over the years, only to have them given back to their abusers with little notice or explanation.

She's the new mom whose child was just diagnosed with a horrendous disease that's flipped her whole world upside down.

The women in this group — and these are real women's stories — are continually being changed by their darkest days.

But this book is not just for one group or the other, this book is for both. My prayer is that the woman in Group 1 is walking away from the end of this book with a new perspective on motherhood, relationships, and family dynamics that may look much different than hers.

I also pray that the woman in Group 2 reads these stories of mine, and she's reminded that there are more of us. That she is not alone, here in her messy in-between, her waiting room. The sharing of our stories is what connects us to each other. It's how we see each other, know each other, respect each other. It's what toughens our skin for the next fire, giving us resiliency with each new chapter.

My story might look different than yours, but pieces of it might be exactly what you need to read to get through this day, or this week, or this season of life that has you questioning everything.

And so what comes next? What can we do with this mess we find ourselves in? How can we wade through the mud and sort through the pieces we're left with?

Great questions, my friend, and not ones that I know the full answers to. My story is not tied up with a bow just yet. I thought I would be writing this book when I was in the clear, on the other side of my middle with a full-circle happy ending. But the truth is, I'm just not. In some ways, my life is more abundant than ever — I

Maybe we don't need to wait for the bow to be tied to unwrap the gift in front of us? Maybe we can relish in the exact season we're in right now? Not worrying about the past or waiting anxiously for the future, but just sitting in the right here, the right now.

can have ice cream for dinner, not shave my legs for a month, and whisk away my adorable pig-tailed sidekick for an afternoon at the movies. But in other ways, my life still feels like it's missing a piece — a partner to share it all with.

So maybe we don't need to wait for the bow to be tied to unwrap the gift in front of us? Maybe we can relish in the exact season we're in right now? Not worrying about the past or waiting anxiously for the future, but just sitting in the right here, the right now.

It's not easy. Poppy and I are both learning patience right now. Her in the I-don't-totally-understand-the-concept-of-time-yet kind of way, and me in the I'm-30-and-have-zero-prospects kind of way. *It never ends, Poppy girl. Sorry 'bout that.* So when I try to explain to her little 3-year-old mind that she needs to be patient and wait nicely for me to get her a fifth cup of goldfish, she replies often with her truest, clearest words: *It's hard waiting, Mama.*

Oh, girl. Don't I know it.

The waiting part is the hardest part. But it can also be a beautiful blossoming part where you come into the woman you were meant to be. Where you can have the time and space to rest, refocus, and come back to the original you. It's like the pause in the waves on the beach before they come crashing back down to meet up with the rest of the ocean. The wave builds up and up, starts to curve in slow motion, and there's that second — that pause — right before it curls all the way over, folding back into itself and washing up on the shore. That pause is where so many of us find ourselves. Hanging in the balance, on the edge of a slow motion curve. We're waiting to come back down and blend back into our own stories.

An email landed in my inbox a few weeks ago from a woman named Val. She had been following my business online for about a year, but I didn't know her, nor had she ever reached out to me personally. But her email is one that I have reread a thousand times. Her words sound off in my head on repeat. She briefly explained how she came to learn about my business and my story, and how she was signing up for my email list when she felt a clear urge that she needed to pray for me. And then she said this:

> While it may feel like you're stuck, you're also positioned. There's not a doubt in my mind if the Lord calls a stranger to pray for you, you are on the brink of better days to come. You have been on God's heart for sure, Kelsey, and He put you on mine to give voice on your behalf. Life is funny sometimes — and by funny, I mean it completely sucks. But there is beauty even in the mess.

Her words — His words — shot straight through to my core, and they've shaken me in the best way possible ever since. *You are on the brink.*

When I feel like I can't make it through until bedtime — you are on the brink.

When I'm so fed up with online dating and Valentine's Day on Instagram makes me want to hurl — you are on the brink.

When I'm questioning why God would drag me through that mud with Dustin, only to give *him* the growing family, and not me — you are on the brink.

And so let me steal Val's prayer, and pass it along to you — whether you're in that Group 1 or Group 2 we talked about earlier. *You are on the brink, sister. You have been on God's heart. There is beauty in your mess.*

———

What are we?

 Strong girls!

 And?

 Brave girls!

Sometimes Poppy says it with gusto, and we flex our muscles for each other as if to prove our worth. Other times she rolls her eyes at me when I start it up, and under her breath mumbles, *strong girls and brave girls,* the way you do when you know your mom is right, but you don't want to admit it.

I don't know exactly how this little back-and-forth started with her, but it must have been at a low point. She had come down off a meltdown and, her cry turned from anger to exhaustion, and I knew it was safe to start reasoning with her. She rarely remembers what sparked her frustration, but after a long talk about channeling our emotions and the big things kids feel in their tiny hearts, I reminded her that we are strong girls, and we are brave girls. The little limerick stuck from then on, and anytime I'd notice her anxiety rising, her fears taking over, I would get down on her level, show her I was there, make her look me in the eye, and like the good nagging mother I am, say *What are we? Remember?*

She is a strong girl. She is a brave girl. And she descends from a long line of strong and brave girls. And as I remind her of that fact daily, I'm also reminding myself. Because even three decades into this whole life gig, it's easy to forget it and even doubt it.

And I'm willing to bet you forget it sometimes, too, so I'll use my best nagging mom voice to remind you.

You *can* do hard things.

You *can* get back up.

You *can* be a strong girl. A brave girl.

THE LeTTERS

One day, you'll be out of this. And all the things you felt — all the places
you went in the dark — will help someone come out of the woods, too.

HANNAH BRENCHER

My people-pleasing heart desperately wants to say, *this book is*
for everyone! It's okay, Men, just skip the birth chapter! But when
I cut to the core of why I wrote this book, I can't deny the truth.

This book is for the girls.

Sorry, boys.

So ladies, listen up. You're at the end of this book, and so now I
consider us girlfriends. I've showed up at your door, dumped all my
crap on your Birkenstocks, and shown you my true colors. You know
the good, the bad, and the ugly — and not just when it comes to marriage or parenting, but when it comes to being a woman whose 180
seconds to land on a life that feels like hers, has felt like an eternity.

Musician Morgan Harper Nichols said it best like this: "Tell the
story of the mountain you climbed. Your words could become a page
in someone else's survival guide." This is not a feminist book; this is

a page from my own story that might serve as a survival guide for one of my girls. *Hint: that's you. I told you about my cervix, so we're friends now, remember?*

And so here, at the end of this survival guide, I'm taking us back to fourth grade for a sec. I'm writing you a letter, folding it up origami style, getting up to pretend I'm sharpening my pencil, and dropping the note in the empty chair next to you. *Wink.* The teacher didn't see that, did she?

Because passing notes is what girls do best.

TO THE GIRL WHO'S STILL SINGLE

————

First of all, sleep in tomorrow for me, will you?! Okay, good, cause I'm tired.

If you were raised in the Christian culture like I was — or if you've frankly just seen any romantic movie ever — then you're probably feeling this pressure to find your person. Society tells us that's the goal. Of course we want to be loved — to be respected, accepted, and known like we talked about earlier. And so the pressure falls on your shoulders to seek that out in a partner. To download all the apps, go on all the dates, give them all a chance. And while that can be fun for a season, and that type of proactiveness has its place, I'm passing you this note to share some good news.

Your worth is not found in another human, *you've had it all along.*

Maybe you've dated a Dustin or a Will or a Ken, Chad, or James. And maybe you've lost yourself a bit in the shuffle. There's a worship song that I've been addicted to lately by Rita Springer called *Defender*. Two lines stick out to me every time I hear it: *When I thought I'd lost me, You knew where I'd left me.*

Not, *You knew the guy who would help me find me.* It just doesn't have the same ring to it, right? The phrasing doesn't quite fit. Oh, and it's just not true. That, too. No, the lyric says, *You knew where I'd left me.* See, you've had your worth all along, maybe you've just lost sight of it.

Having a partner might not be the ultimate goal of life, but from one single lady to another, I'm well aware that it's a dream. You want a built-in person to share your life with, and there's nothing wrong with that at all. The thing I want to drill into your head here is that there is also nothing wrong with *you*. Take advantage of this single season you find yourself in. For me, that looks like traveling with friends and family, exploring places I've always wanted to go, even if it's by myself. Stepping out of my comfort zone and into coffee shops with new friends. Caring for myself with a comfy robe and a glass of wine for no particular reason. And setting high standards with a clear head for when my heart feels flustered standing in front of someone tall, dark, and handsome.

My dear friend Adie is 39 and single. She lives life more fully than anyone I know. She is a light when she walks into a room. She is glowing with a presence and a laugh that is infectious. She is quite literally, the most interesting woman in the world. She has traveled to every corner of the globe, had every type of job you can imagine, and she could probably make friends with a brick wall. I remember sitting on the beach with her one morning when I was visiting her in California. We were watching the surfers ride the morning waves, and I'll stop there because this Missouri girl knows nothing of the surfing lingo. But as we were walking back to her car, and I was brushing sand off my feet, Adie said something that's stuck in my head ever since. She said she loves the feeling of sand in her sheets. Like, when she crawls in bed at night, slips her toes down into her cold sheets, and she feels little bits of sand under the covers. "That's how I know it's been a day well spent," she said smiling. A reminder of a day at her favorite place: the sea.

She thrives without a partner, but I know she craves one at the same time because of our candid conversations. So listen up, friends, you can have both. You can rejoice in the fact that you don't have to share the remote, *and* long for a warm body on the other end of the couch to watch just one more episode of *The Office* with you. You can eat copious amounts of pasta with your brother in Italy, *and* still wish to come back someday with a man who is not related to you. The thriving and the craving can co-exist, and this is your permission to let them.

So about a month later when I was in Florida with my family for vacation, and I slipped into bed quietly, (trying not to wake Poppy asleep next to me), I felt it. Little bits of sand met my toes at the end of my bed, and I smiled. Adie was right. I had spent the day at the beach with some of my favorite people. And while the kid may have melted down, and my period may have decided to start two weeks early, and while I may have dreamed of having a partner to watch the sunset with, the sand in my sheets at the end of the day reminded me that it was still a day well spent.

It's hard waiting, Mama.

Me and Poppy know this too well. I get it, because I'm in this boat with you. But tucked inside this note I'm passing you is a permission slip — permission to feel the sand in your sheets. To spend less of your days waiting around and more of your days finding where you left yourself.

Because remember what you are? You are a strong girl, a brave girl.

TO THE GIRL WHO'S GETTING MARRIED

————

Well, congratulations are in order! You've got the ring on your finger, you're knee deep in white dresses, and you lay awake at night thinking about place settings. I've been there, too, and the anxious anticipation is something that still makes me smile, despite my unexpected ending. And I know, *I know,* who wants to take marriage advice from the divorced girl? Trust me, this is not lost on me. But humor me for a second. Smile and nod politely as I pass this note from simply one woman to another.

Use the stories in this book, the broken relationship that I am left with, and let it serve as your motivation for what *not* to do. Be honest with each other. Don't keep score. Serve each other as equals. Know that it will get hard. Do not feel shame when a piece of you wants to throw in the towel. But when you're holding the towel in your hand, ready to throw it as hard as you can, remember this book. Remember the number of lives that that one decision affects. All those names on your guest list — use them. When things get hard, call on them to be your village. Let them help you and rally with you and be your reminder of what they witnessed on your wedding day.

This letter is a short one, for obvious reasons. But I couldn't let you slip under the radar without a reminder that you may need just as badly as the other women reading this book: You are a strong girl, a brave girl.

TO THE GIRL WHO'S GETTING DIVORCED

———

Girl. Oh, girl. I am so very sorry. Divorce is so painful and alienating and I wouldn't wish it on my worst enemy. This season you find yourself in is confusing and uncertain, but please don't lose heart. I'm passing you a note today with a simple nugget of wisdom that came directly from my mother on the night my husband left me — *You are stronger than you think you are.*

When I sat with my mom and cried over my marriage and the thought of my child never knowing her parents together, she reminded me, *you are stronger than you think you are.*

When I would leave meetings with my ex-husband during my pregnancy where we discussed baby names and visitation schedules, and I questioned if I could do this for the next 18 years, I tried to remember, *you are stronger than you think you are.*

When I sat in my attorney's office signing divorce papers, with a 3-week old baby asleep in the car seat next to me, I said through gritted teeth, *you are stronger than you think you are.*

Divorce is a breaking apart of something that was once whole. When you're left standing in an empty house with your half of the whole, it can feel like every ounce of strength has been sucked out of you. So if you need to hear this, and I'm 99% sure you do, let me have the honor of passing it on from my mama: *You are stronger than you think you are.* You may feel unsure at this new starting line, back at Square One, but at the finish line you'll look back and see how far you ran and the hurtles you jumped to get there.

In Amy Poehler's fabulously hilarious and inspiring book *Yes, Please,* she only briefly mentions her divorce with one simple statement that rings so true: "I don't think a 10-year marriage constitutes failure." So many people would define divorce as a *failed marriage.* Please don't buy in to this. It's an ending, not a failing. It's the closing of a chapter, not a burning of the whole book. Marriage is hard. You figured out how *not* to do it. That's not a failure, that's a chance to try again.

On the days when it feels like the world is crumbling around you, please don't forget it — you are a strong girl and a very, very brave girl.

TO THE GIRL WHO'S ABOUT TO BECOME A MOTHER

———

Well, well, well, the stork is flying in! No matter the circumstances, a new life is something to celebrate, so pop the sparkling grape juice and let's toast! To sleepless nights, never peeing alone, and wiping poop off places you didn't think poop could reach. Cheers to babies!

Okay, okay, those aren't the most glorious moments of motherhood, but they are a reality, so prepare yourself, Mama. Aside from the bodily fluids, you have a world full of more pleasant things to look forward to, too. You know the ones — the soft, squishy baby skin that's impossible not to squeeze; the tiniest little baby socks that make laundry folding a little sweeter; and the coos and caws of a new little mind learning about the big world surrounding her. Becoming a mother is one of the most overwhelmingly joyful and terrifying experiences on this Earth.

If you're pregnant, you will push a whole other human being out of *your* human being body — how crazy is that?! And if you're adopting or fostering or using surrogacy, it's even more so! One day it's just you, and the next day another little human being is dropped in your lap.

No matter how you arrived at motherhood, in the beginning, you'll have no clue what you're doing. It may take several months to start feeling your feet planted firmly underneath you again. And then four years later, 12 years later, in their last year of high school, you'll still be trying to figure each other out. Easier, then harder, then easier, then harder again, remember?

But in the midst of all of that chaos, know this: it is *honorable* work, being a mother. You may not feel that at 3:00 am for the 48th night in a row, so maybe tattoo it on your forehead so you don't forget. It will not be easy, but it will become your greatest achievement. If there's one simple note that I could pass along to you as you set out on this rollercoaster journey to motherhood, it is this: you are a strong girl, a brave girl.

TO THE GIRL WHO'S RAISING HER KIDS WITHOUT A PARTNER

Your letter might be the longest, lucky you, because this is my camp.

You know it too well — single parenting is lonely. You don't have a built-in helper, you don't tag-team it, you don't get many breaks, and not many other mamas really "get it." So I'm passing you this note, reminding you that you are not alone.

This book was written for women of all kinds who find themselves in need of a fresh perspective, a shoulder to cry on, or a girlfriend to laugh with, but this book was written mostly for you. The single mother who is taking it one day at a time.

So first of all, just breathe. Not all mama moments are pleasant, as you well know. It's unbelievably draining doing this job alone, and not very motivating to pull all the weight like that. It can easily lead to some bad attitudes and tempers when your mini-me is driving you crazy. So lay this book down for a second, and just breathe. You're doing a good job. You're doing the job you were made for. It takes a special breed of mama to go it alone, and you have been strong enough and brave enough to take that on. I pray it is just a season for you, like I pray for myself. I pray you get a helper soon, but in the meantime, I pray that you relish in it. I want you to squeeze your kids and savor the fact that you get them all to yourself, and they get your undivided attention. What a gift for your kids to see such a pillar of strength and perseverance, day in and day out. Your hard work is not going unnoticed, I promise you.

Second, and it can seem a little contrary, but know that you can't do it *all* alone. The overused phrase is overused because it's true — *it takes a village*. So when your tempers flare or you feel a good ugly cry coming on, use a lifeline — phone a friend. Text your child-less best friend, "Hey, just so you know my kid just dumped out her entire dinner onto the floor, so enjoy your quiet evening to yourself tonight." Snap a picture of your upside down, pee-stained couch and post it on Instagram sharing your potty training woes with the world. Not to seek pity, but to find encouragement in your community, in your tribe of witnesses. Chances are, other mothers will see it — mothers of all kinds — and they're probably tired of being a mom right now, too. Commiserate together. Ask for help. Learn to laugh at yourself and this weird circumstance that you're in. Laughter can truly be the best medicine. The other day, my mom was visiting for the weekend, and as I was cooking the three of us dinner, she asked, "Do you cook dinner every night?" Without missing a beat, I replied, "Well, who else is gonna do it?" In print, that sounds really cynical, but in the moment, we laughed until we cried. Single mom jokes — they're a thing!

Day-to-day, you might be calling the shots by yourself, but you are not alone. There are communities and pockets of people exactly like you, with the same struggles and trials, all of us navigating the worlds of parenting together. You may be driving the ship alone, but you've got people around you to help you steer.

Thirdly, record your story. When I think about the most trying times with Poppy, I think about sleepless nights in the newborn stage. I think about teething. I think about taking her to family functions when she was so not in the mood, and we'd both leave in tears. Even though these memories aren't the most positive, they're still a part of my story and my journey as a mother. And for that reason, I think it's important to write them down. Sometimes just for myself to look back on the next time I'm having a rough day. When you look back at these not-so-pleasant moments, even just a few months from now, you'll see how far you've come and what you've been able to survive. You'll recognize your own strength — because it can be so hard to see it in the moment. And you'll feel like you can do anything. In the same way, document the happy moments. They remind you that after this season of teething or tantrums, there *will* be a funny moment or sweet gesture that will snap you back to reality; a subtle reminder that this whole mom thing is totally worth it.

Take care of yourself, Mama. Ask for help when you need it. It is not a sign of weakness, it's a sign of bravery. Because remember what you are? You are a strong girl, a brave girl.

TO THE GIRL WHO'S HAPPILY MARRIED WITH 2.5 KIDS

———

Stop what you're doing and send your partner a sweet text, because having that built-in support is a blessing that should not be taken for granted. Ok, now back to this note I'm passing you.

My hope as you read these stories and held space for what I wanted to share in this book, is that you would find nuggets of encouragement and motivation in these words, simply from one mom to another. We're all in this together, and no one's story of motherhood is better or worse than another's. Like I mentioned in the last chapter, may this book be the shift in perspective that allows you to choose gratitude. An angle on marriage and motherhood that maybe you've never been exposed to.

That's not to say that being married with 2.5 kids is all rainbows and unicorns. You could be passing the kid baton back and forth everyday without a second to spare for yourselves. Your spouse could travel a lot or work late nights or just feel unavailable sometimes. When I was living in Nashville, I joined a small group for single moms, and after the leader decided she had too much on her plate (single mom problems, can I get an amen?!), another mom in the group stepped up to host us — but she was married. At first I was skeptical, but Megan ended up being the glue for all of us. Her husband was in the music industry, in true Nashville form, so he was on the road for several months at a time. She straddled that line of being alone and having a partner. She understood both sides. Even when a fancy piece of paper says you have a helper, it can still be a one-woman show.

There's a lot of pressure that comes with being a wife and a mother at the same time, and honestly, that's a perspective that I've ironically never experienced. And to be even more honest, sometimes I'm terrified of it. I've only ever done this job alone, so I can't imagine what it's like to share the responsibilities with another person full-time. That might get an eye-roll or two, but it's the truth. Because with a shared responsibility comes some not so pleasant side dishes like resentment, jealousy, and keeping score. It's just further proof that as mothers, we *need* each other's stories. We need to share in our struggles and savor our victories with each other. Because every mother, every wife, is fighting her own battle, and she needs to know that she is not alone in it.

And so here is your reminder, as you continue learning how to balance your wife duties with your mom duties with all the other duties on your plate right now — you are a strong girl, a brave girl. You've got this, Mama.

TO THE GIRL WHO'S WATCHING HER KIDS START THEIR OWN LIVES (YES I CAN CALL YOU GIRL, GIRRRRL)

———

You didn't think you'd sneak through this chapter without your own letter, did you? This will be another shorty, because again, this is not my arena. But you were a young mother once, too, married or not. You may not be in that messy in-between phase of motherhood anymore, but being a mother-turned-friend, and even a grandmother, can come with its own set of unique challenges. And so, I hope you've seen some of yourself in these stories I've shared. I hope you've read this account of another mother, and remembered your own moments in the trenches. I hope you looked up from this book and smiled at where you are now. You're on the other side of it. You raised children, you served your time. What a feat, well done! Huge congratulations are in order for you, Mama.

So as you step into this new stage of motherhood that looks a lot different than the days of potty training and bedtime stories, may you be open to the new things you'll find. May you impart your finishing wisdom on your sons and daughters, but may you honor the journey that they are just beginning as parents.

I can only imagine what an incredible, full-circle thing it is to witness your children have children of their own. And you know all too well that with such a beautiful cycle beginning again, there's bound to be unexpected turns and some messy in-betweens. So when you find yourself there, remember what you are, and always have been — you are a strong girl, a brave girl.

TO THE GIRL WHO JUST NEEDS TO HEAR IT

————

I don't know where you are or what you're going through. Maybe you're grieving something, waiting on something, holding too tightly to something, or maybe you're just at capacity and looking for a way out. You're sitting in your messy in-between, unsure of what's next. I'm right there with you, so I'm passing this note over to you.

There's a distinct, liberating power in saying *nope, I can't do it all.*

It is not a failure to not complete something, it's simply accepting the reality that you are not a superhuman. (Good news, none of us are. You're in the right place.) In fact, it's inspiring for others to see someone else bravely admitting they can't do it all. It can give them the courage to do the same.

This year, I started doing hot yoga once a week, and recently the teacher said something that stuck with me. She paced the room, talking through each flow of poses, encouraging us to listen to our bodies — specifically if our bodies were saying *no.* Your decision to *not* do a pose or take a break could be exactly what the person next to you needs to see, in order for them to listen to their own body. Their body could be saying *no*, but they're having a hard time listening to it. They may need to see five people in the room say *no* before they have the courage to say *no*, too. You could be number five.

Her words were a far cry from the intense workout scenes you see on *The Biggest Loser* — *push harder, shove the pain down, white knuckle through it,* they shout. And while that can be sage advice for a weight loss reality TV show — or say, childbirth — it's not a way to prove your strength. It's a way to throw out your back, that's what.

You can't do it all. You can't be everything for everyone. You can say *no*. You can be strong enough and brave enough to untangle yourself from this pose you're trying to hold and take a break. And that might be what everyone *actually* needs to see from you. To give them the guts to slow down and do the same.

This book has been my untangling. I unraveled myself onto these pages and recognized that I can't do it all, I don't have everything figured out, and I'm still in my messy in-between. I'm learning to be okay with this middle phase, and my hope is that this book has encouraged you to do the same.

Because no matter where you find yourself, remember what you are? You are a strong girl, a brave girl.

TO THE PARTNER I HOPE TO HAVE SOMEDAY

————

I don't know you, yet, but I think about you a lot. I think about the smiling moments we'll have, the sweeping gestures and the big Jack-and-Rebecca-Pearson-style love we'll share. But in the same breath,

I'm grieving. I grieve the loss of your witness — that by the time our paths cross, you will have missed this beautifully wild season of Poppy's life, her earliest years. There will always be memories that are only mine to remember. I'll tell you about our life before you, but it won't quite be the same. They'll be stories that you'll come to know by heart, but ones that you didn't get to participate in.

There will always be holes, even though you will fill in so much, and so I ask you this one thing: be patient with us. I've only ever known her with me, and she's only ever known me with her. We're a package deal. Two for one. We carry some baggage, and there's a twinge of heartache that still seeps into our simplest of moments. Bear with us as we learn to let you in.

But there is one really important thing you'll need to know about us if you want a place in our hearts: we are strong girls, we are brave girls, and we host regular dance parties in the kitchen, so I hope you've got some moves.

TO POPPY

———

To my sweet Penelope Rose. How do you squeeze so much love out of me each day, and even more the next? You are my heart outside of my body. Even after you finally go to bed on the hardest of days, I find myself scrolling through pictures of you on my phone. Missing you, just one room over.

Sometimes I feel like I've already let you down. I'm sorry we couldn't bring you into a family where you could enjoy both of your parents at the same time. Going from Mommy's house to Daddy's house to Mommy's house to Daddy's house, it makes you tired — I know this because you've told me. I'm sorry we've made you go through these transitions and swapping houses and feeling these big feelings that a little girl should never have to feel.

But there are silver linings to the hard things, Sweet P. *Silver linings* is a hard thing to explain, but it's like happy parts of a sad story. Your happy part is that you have a lot of people who love you. Your happy part is that you'll have a bigger family than most kids. I can already see that you are resilient like your Mommy, and goofy like your Daddy.

And my silver lining — my happy part — is you. I get to be your mom, and that is a privilege I will forever be honored to have. You sometimes ask me if being a mommy is hard work, and of course the answer is *yes*. But you're my little reminder that we can do hard things. Thank you for being patient with me, and loving me unconditionally, even on my worst days. The compassion you are able to show in your little heart is astounding and wildly humbling.

And no matter what, my sweet 'Nelope, never forget what you are — you are a strong girl, and you are a brave girl. And I love you so very much.

TO ME

———

Hey, girl. *I know this is weird, me talking to me, but bear with me for this last little sec.*

A few weeks ago you started watching a TV show called *The Marvelous Mrs. Maisel.* The pivotal scene that set the stage for the whole series was in that first episode when Mrs. Maisel walks in on her husband stuffing clothes into a suitcase — *her* suitcase, mind you — and spewing the words, *I want a divorce.*

"Did you ever think you were supposed to be something, and then suddenly you're not?" he asked her frantically while he packed. There was a nice, long pause after his question as they both tried to wrap their heads around what was suddenly unfolding in front of them.

And she calmly and matter-of-factly responds, "Yes. Married."

I don't know if you remember lying in bed late that night watching that scene on the glow of your laptop, but it was like watching an old home video. It was comically close to home. You laughed out loud for a good two minutes remembering your own *yes, married* moment. It wasn't that long ago, but it was roughly four Kelsey's ago. It was a moment that seemed like it could only be the stuff of dramedy television writers. But it was your actual life, your actual marriage. I know sometimes you pinch yourself thinking maybe all that chaos was just a terrible dream, and you'll wake up back in that house on Stewart Street, him snoring away next to you.

But given the choice between the two, I know you would choose your *yes, married* moment every time. It gave you Poppy, it gave you freedom, and it gave you the chance to share a story that a lot of women needed to hear in order to keep moving through their own.

Look around you now, Kels. You're sitting in a nice hotel room in Bentonville, Arkansas with a bottle of wine, some fancy potato chips that you've deemed too spicy, and a box of Thin Mints. You turn 30 next week, and while I know it's disappointing that you're not quite where you thought you'd be at 30, look at how far you've come. You're finishing that book you always said you were going to write. These are literally the last words you're typing on the screen. Can you believe it? Can you believe we're here? When I say we, I mean you there in the hotel, and me here in the future looking back at Hotel You, thinking *girrrrl, you have no idea what's coming.* You're on the brink of something, remember? You are on God's heart, and He has not forgotten about you.

So, close your eyes and feel Poppy's sticky little hands cupping your face as she mimics you. She won't let you forget it, because you won't let her either: *You are a strong girl, a brave girl.*

ACKNOWLEDGEMENTS

A million thank you's are in order, so I'll try to get through these before the orchestra cuts me off.

Thank you to my high school English teacher turned editor, Alicia Kelley, for all your hard work on this project, for being tender with something that is oh so personal, and for encouraging me when I've second guessed myself, and third guessed myself, and fourth, and on and on. You helped polish this sucker off, and I'm so grateful this book enabled us to cross paths again.

Thank you to my parents for being so unbelievably supportive in the writing of this book, but more importantly in the living out of this story. You both were my safe place in your own ways, and I'm so grateful me and Poppy get to call you our own.

Thank you to my brothers, Grant and Taylor, and my sister-in-law Sheila. You guys have kept me grounded, kept me laughing, and kept my head on straight. Sheila, thanks for being the very first person to finish the book; Grant, thanks for counting how many times I used "special words"; and Taylor, thanks for complaining about how long the email was that I sent the manuscript in. Let's all make that sibling trip happen already, mmmkay?

Thank you to my dearest friends, Kayla and Brandon, for how you loved me through all the ugly crying, fed me countless meals around your table, and most of all, have loved Poppy like your own.

Thank you to my pals Jamie and Phyllis for cheering me on every step of the way, and adding to my to do list that afternoon in Philly, "Write the book already."

Thank you to my Nashville girls — Megan, Steph, and Heather — for seeing me through that crazy season, and letting me crash your dinners when I'm back in town.

Thank you times infinity to my favorite ladies to spend a Tuesday night with — Ana, Amber, Emma, Emily, Jenn, Karen, Kate, Katie, KaTrina, Kesha, Leah, Lindsay, Mara, Michelle, Morgan, Sarah, and Shailey. Thanks for letting me spill my guts, not running away from it, and including me in this special thing you've got going.

Thank you to my Pensacola girls — Brittany, Erin, Janet, Jenn, Kristin, Mallory, and Stephanie — for helping me hash out early details in the writing process, and all yelling "YES!" in unison when I mentioned this little idea I had for the title.

Thank you to countless others who helped me flesh out ideas, organize thoughts, and talk through concepts — Adie, Anna, Ashley, Christian, Erica, and Jessica, to name a few.

Thank you to the women who have shared their stories with me, and in doing so, encouraged me to keep sharing mine.

And thank you Poppy for being my best little friend, my cover art painter, and all those other gushy mom things I want to put here, but will refrain. I love you, little bird.

 @PAPERANDOATS

@PAPERANDOATS

/PAPERANDOATS

Kelsey Baldwin is the founder and designer behind Paper + Oats, an online resource for creative entrepreneurs looking to do business on their own terms. She helps fellow creatives organize, design, and market their digital products, so they can share what they know, and look good doing it.

2013 was a major turning point in her life as she found herself single, pregnant, and suddenly needing to google divorce lawyers. She soon welcomed her favorite tiny human, Poppy. This not-so-little detour was certainly unconventional, and lit a fire under her as she poured herself into Paper + Oats, growing it into the business it is today. What started as just a few printable planners on Etsy and a handful of freelance clients, has grown into a brand that blends thoughtful design and practical organization into educational tools for creatives who sell digital products — proving that yes, you can get back up after adversity, and do great things in the aftermath. [Insert fist pump here.]

She started writing about her divorce and life as a single mother in 2015, and was overwhelmed by the response from other women who were struggling through divorce, single motherhood, or just motherhood in general. Her *why* came into view for Paper + Oats, and she became an advocate for women learning to sustain themselves and gain independence through online business.

When she's not designing or writing or wearing all those other businessy hats, she's usually walking down to the ice cream shop with Poppy, vacuuming up enough dog hair to make another border collie, or painting just about any surface in her 1930s bungalow in Missouri.

To learn more about the creative programs, resources, and articles from Kelsey at Paper + Oats, check out www.paperandoats.com.

13544132R00153

Made in the USA
Lexington, KY
01 November 2018